Living into Lent

Donald K. McKim

WJK WESTMINSTER
JOHN KNOX PRESS
LOUISVILLE • KENTUCKY

20 21 22 23 24 25 26 27 28 29—10 9 8 7 6 5 4 3 2 1

Book design by Jeanne Williams
Cover design by Marc Whitaker/MTWdesign.net

Library of Congress Cataloging-in-Publication Data
Names: McKim, Donald K., author.
Title: Living into Lent / Donald K. McKim.
Description: First. | Louisville, Kentucky : Westminster John Knox Press, 2020. | Originally published : Louisville, Kentucky : Witherspoon Press, ©2013. | Includes bibliographical references. | Summary: "The Lenten journey is a shared journey-Christians join with others along the way of faith, following Jesus and seeking to live out the will and purpose of God. Living into Lent, written by noted theologian, educator, and author Donald K. McKim, sets aside time during the Lenten season for readers to reflect on their Christian identities, listen to God's Word and will, and engage in practices that deepen the Christian experience through discipleship. Whether used for congregational study or personal reflection, each reading features Scripture, devotion, theological quote, response, and prayer. Theological quotes, drawn from the history of the Reformed church, will help readers better understand God's Word and its implications for the Lenten journey. Readings are enhanced by a seven-session study guide and questions for conversation"-- Provided by publisher.
Identifiers: LCCN 2019035628 (print) | LCCN 2019035629 (ebook) | ISBN 9780664265403 (paperback) | ISBN 9781611649796 (ebook)
Subjects: LCSH: Lent--Textbooks.
Classification: LCC BV85 .M385 2020 (print) | LCC BV85 (ebook) | DDC 242/.34--dc23
LC record available at https://lccn.loc.gov/2019035628
LC ebook record available at https://lccn.loc.gov/2019035629

Most Westminster John Knox Press books are available at special quantity discounts when purchased in bulk by corporations, organizations, and special-interest groups. For more information, please e-mail SpecialSales@wjkbooks.com.

A Lenten Journey

This book is written as a resource for those who want to focus on Christian living and reflection during the season of Lent.

Lent is the forty-day period in the Christian year that begins with Ash Wednesday and extends to Holy Saturday, the day of the Great Vigil of Easter, which is the day before Easter Sunday. Lent is comprised of weekdays, with the Sundays in Lent being specially marked. Thus, the forty days begin with the four weekdays during the week of Ash Wednesday, and continue through six weeks of six days each, making the forty days of Lent. Devotions for the Sundays in Lent are included in this book as well.

Lent has always been a time of special devotion for Christians. It is a time for reflecting on our Christian lives, listening to God's word and will for us, and engaging in practices that can deepen our Christian experience. The meditations that follow seek to honor these impulses and provide ways of reflecting on dimensions of Christian faith that can be meaningful and significant for us.

These devotions can be used privately or in a group setting. We Christians do not live out our Christian walk by ourselves. We do so in the company of the committed, the church. We are joined to Jesus Christ by faith in and through the church. God calls and works through people in this world; and the church is the people of God who are sent by God in mission and ministry. The personal dimensions of our faith come to us in the midst of those sisters and brothers in Christ who share common faith and with whom we share our commitments to love, justice, and peace in the Christian community. What is personal in these devotions is also corporate. What is true for us in our own Christian experience resonates with others and is lived out by others as well. Therefore, our Lenten journey is very much a shared journey. We join others along the way of faith, following Jesus, and seeking to live out the will and purposes of God for our lives.

Ways to Use This Book

This book provides devotions to be used during the period of Lent. The book can be used in different ways.

Each devotion features a Scripture passage, a devotion title, a biblical text for the devotion drawn from the Scripture passage, a theological quote, a devotional essay, an Action Step, and a prayer. The theological quotations are drawn from the history of the church and are used to help us better understand the Scripture text and its implications for life. The quotes do not take the place of the Scripture; they help open its meaning so the Word of God can reach us and move us.

Each of the seven weekly sections has a theme: following Jesus, meditating, praying, loving, thanking, enacting, and gathering at the cross. All of these themes, of course, are intermixed in the lives we live. But in Lent we can focus on aspects of our Christian life in a more concentrated way. Each theme focuses on a dimension of our Lenten journey with appropriate devotions.

Readers can use the book in one of two ways:

1. Reading the devotions chronologically, beginning with Ash Wednesday and finishing on Holy Saturday. This enables a concentration on the theme of each week.
2. Reading a devotion from a different segment of the book on the different days of a week throughout each week in Lent. This practice can begin during the First Week in Lent and follow through Holy Week. This enables one to experience the various themes throughout the course of each week.

Either approach can be used for individual reading or for group use of this book.

The seven study sessions are designed for groups who wish to do further reflections on the devotions.

I am grateful to be able to offer *Living into Lent* to the church.

This project is published by CMP of the Presbyterian Church (U.S.A.) and is written from my context as a Reformed theologian in the Presbyterian tradition. But the themes of Lent go beyond any single, denominational tradition. So this is a book for the ecumenical church and for all Christian believers who want to deepen their devotional lives during Lent.

One of my passions is to retrieve and try to revitalize the Christian theological tradition and to communicate insights from the great theologians of the past into the life of the church today. I have structured the devotions with theological quotes from past and present theologians and theological documents. These quotes, I trust, will help to illuminate the Scripture text and to provide a source for meditation in themselves. To me, it is always the question from the book of Ezekiel: "Can these bones live?" (Ezekiel 37:3). Can the old writings and theologians communicate meaningfully, with vitality, for our Christian faith today? I hope this smattering of theological quotes will do so during Lent.

My thanks go to Clare Lewis and Mark Hinds of CMP, who kindly invited and supported this work. Mark Hinds gave excellent editorial advice and provided the study sessions. I deeply appreciate their ministries and friendship. As always, my wife, LindaJo, has been lovingly supportive. Our sons and their families—Stephen, Caroline, and Maddie; and Karl and Lauren—bring blessings and joy to life together.

This book is gratefully dedicated to the historic ministries of the Presbyterian Church (U.S.A.).

Donald K. McKim

Chapter 1

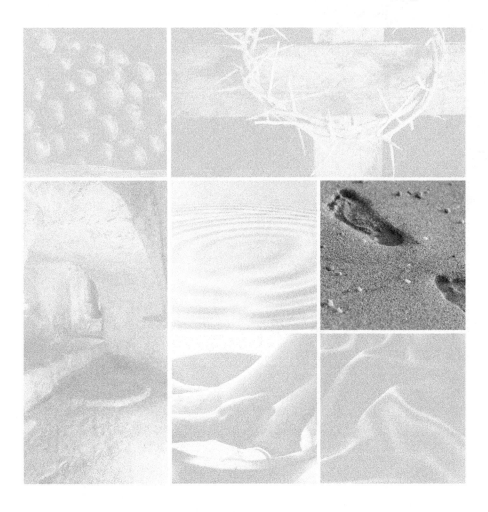

Following Jesus
(Week of Ash Wednesday)

Following Jesus

If we want a capsule definition of Christian life and experience, we can do no better than these two words: following Jesus. These simple words introduce us to a never-ending adventure of moving through life in the ways our Lord and Savior, Jesus Christ, points us to go. Our path will not be easy. However, we do not follow Jesus alone. We have the gift of the Holy Spirit, the care of the Christian community—the church—and the presence of Jesus himself as our divine companions.

The stories of Jesus calling his first disciples to "Follow me" (Matthew 4:18–22) are astounding. The record is that "immediately" they left what they were doing and followed him. We wonder why. What prompted them immediately to leave all? Did they know what they were getting into by traipsing after the itinerant preacher who would change their lives in such dramatic ways? Their decision gave them a new self-identity. Their adventure of faith led them through trials, as well as joys. They gave to Jesus an allegiance, a commitment, and obedience unlike those given to anyone else. Their response to Jesus' call to follow is what made all the difference in the lives of the disciples.

Jesus' call still comes to us. He invites us to respond, to be his followers, to commit our lives to him, to live in obedience to his will and his way. Our Lenten journey is a time of focusing strongly on what it means to be a disciple, or follower, of Jesus Christ. Discipleship begins with a step of faith. We move to new understandings of ourselves. We follow the ways Jesus points us toward. We experience the joys of living in Christ and of Christ living in us (Galatians 2:20). We hear Jesus say: "Follow me."

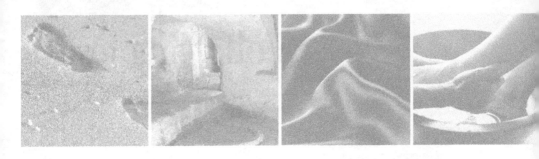

Ash Wednesday

They left everything and followed him.

Luke 5:11

Pray
O Lord Jesus Christ, be with me, and lead me in your way, helping me to trust you as we go. Amen.

Read
Luke 5:1–11

Reflect
God has come down to us, has taken our nature, and is become one of us, that he might be our companion.

—Jonathan Edwards[1]

Consider
"Christ Our Companion" (p. 5)

Action Step
Think of how you experience the companionship of Jesus.

Christ Our Companion

We begin our Lenten journey with Ash Wednesday. On this day we look beyond ourselves to God, who calls us to travel as disciples of Jesus Christ through the following weeks, to the cross on Good Friday and beyond, to the message of resurrection on Easter.

Like the first disciples whom Jesus called, we respond to the voice of Jesus, who says, "Follow me" (Mark 1:17). We too are called to be ones who have "left everything and followed him."

We start on our Lenten journey. However, we do not travel alone. The good news is that God is with us, every step of the way. God is with us in Jesus Christ, every step of the way. This is the resource we in the church have for our living into Lent. We have a companion. Jesus Christ, our divine companion, is with us.

Jonathan Edwards helps us recognize that the great God has come down to us and become one of us, taking our nature. Why? So that Jesus Christ may be our companion—through Lent and through all our days.

We step out in Lent, turning from our own ways to the way of Jesus. We follow Jesus as his disciples. But as we do, Jesus is with us. He is one of us, human to the core. He understands us even as he stands under us, supporting us at every step. We share fellowship in him and with him. We are not alone and need not be afraid. In Jesus, we have joy in the journey!

> **We step out in Lent, turning from our own ways to the way of Jesus.**

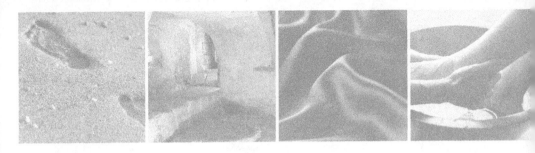

Thursday

But I have called you friends.
John 15:15

Pray
Dear Jesus, show me the directions you want me to follow and help me when I stumble. Amen.

Read
John 15:12–17

Reflect
The living Christ still has two hands, one to point the way, and the other held out to help us along. . . . And we are assured, as we set out on the journey, that he is with us always, even unto the end of the world.

—T. W. Manson[2]

Consider
"The Two Hands of Christ" (p. 7)

Action Step
Consider the two hands of Christ and reflect on where you believe Christ is pointing your life. Also reflect on how you experience the help Jesus brings on your journey.

The Two Hands of Christ

One of our beloved hymns is "What a Friend We Have in Jesus." In one of the stanzas, we sing: "Can we find a friend so faithful, who will all our sorrows share?" Friendship with Jesus is a precious gift. We know Jesus Christ as a person, as our friend. He is a real presence in our lives. We are united with Jesus by faith; and by faith, we experience the presence of Christ in real and meaningful ways.

We are united with Jesus by faith; and by faith, we experience the presence of Christ in real and meaningful ways.

T. W. Manson has shown us the two hands of Christ. One points the way; the other helps us along the way. This is exactly what we need in our Christian lives, isn't it? We need to know the way, the path, the direction to follow in life. Jesus is "the way" (John 14:6) and he points his way to us. He invites us to follow his way, with him.

We also need Jesus' help along our way. This is a great comfort in our friendship with Jesus. He is faithful to us, he shares our sorrow, he picks us up when we fall, he is with us always (Matthew 28:20). If we had this assurance from any other friend, we might hope for the best. Others can disappoint us, leave us to face difficulties on our own, and even abandon us. But not Jesus. He is joined with us and is our true guide and friend.

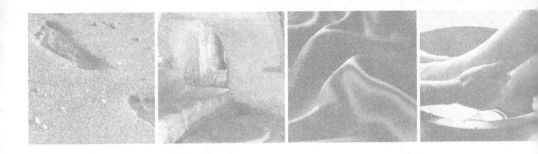

Friday

He went away grieving, for he had many possessions.

Matthew 19:22

Pray
O Lord Jesus, help us know the opportunity of discipleship so that as we follow you, we will experience the true life you want us to have as your disciples. Amen.

Read
Matthew 19:16–26

Reflect
The following of Christ therefore is not a privilege of the group of disciples.... Being a disciple ... is a special task, a special destiny, a special promise; a special opportunity which is missed by the young man whose riches prevent him from following Jesus.

—Hans Küng[3]

Consider
"The Opportunity of Discipleship" (p. 9)

Action Step
Contemplate what possessions you have that might be hindering you from fuller service to Christ. Decide whether you can let go of some of these.

The Opportunity of Discipleship

The philosopher René Descartes coined the phrase "I think, therefore I am." If I realize I am thinking, I must exist. In our acquisitive society, we tend to say, "I possess, therefore I am." Our lives and possessions are so intertwined that what we have may define who we are.

In the end, the rich young ruler, who came to Jesus, could not part with his possessions in order to respond to Jesus' call to follow him. The possessions prevented his discipleship. The lure of what he possessed kept him from what he could become. So he went away, grieving. Perhaps he had a vision of a greater life, as a disciple. But he was never to know what was possible. His personal wealth choked his opportunity for discipleship.

Hans Küng reminds us that being a disciple of Jesus is special in many ways. A special mission claims our whole lives and gives focus to all we think, say, and do. Discipleship opens up a destiny we could never know otherwise. It holds an assurance of Christ's presence with us that is a promise that can be trusted. Discipleship is a special opportunity that holds open for us the best life possible—not a life that makes us rich and famous, but a life that is eternal—the true life in God we were created to live and enjoy.

> **Discipleship opens up a destiny we could never know otherwise.**

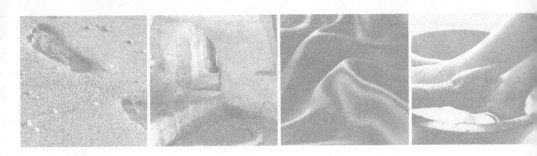

Saturday

And he said to him, "Follow me." And he got up and followed him.

Mark 2:14

Pray
Help us to know the joy of being your disciples, O Christ. Help us to face the future with the assurance of your mercy. Amen.

Read
Mark 2:13–17

Reflect
Only Jesus Christ, who bids us follow him, knows the journey's end. But we know that it will be a road of boundless mercy. Discipleship means joy.

—Dietrich Bonhoeffer[4]

Consider
"The Joy of Discipleship" (p. 11)

Action Step
List ways in which your following Jesus brings you joy. Think of times when Christ's mercy has brought you joy.

The Joy of Discipleship

We often like to know the end from the beginning. Some folks will turn to the final pages of a mystery novel to find out "Who dunnit?" right away, so they can follow the character through the plot of the story.

In the bigger picture of life, we would all like to know "how it ends" for us. But this is a mystery, unknown through all our years. We do not and cannot know how our life will end, as we move along. That is reserved for the final chapter of our life's story.

Dietrich Bonhoeffer encourages us to recognize, as disciples of Jesus Christ, that Christ knows our journey's end. He sees our destination and guides us along the way, pointing us, helping us, supporting us. Through it all, Christ offers mercy and forgiveness for our sins and failures, for what we have done and what we have left undone. Bonhoeffer says Christ's mercy is boundless. We can face any future, secure in Christ's mercy. This is our great need— and what Jesus gives us.

> **Christ offers mercy and forgiveness for our sins and failures, for what we have done and what we have left undone.**

So no wonder, as Bonhoeffer notes, "discipleship means joy." It is the joy of life lived to the fullest in service to Christ. It is lived in freedom to love and help others, to extend Christ's mercy, and to find the true life Christ came to bring. As we respond to the call to follow Jesus, our joy will be everlasting.

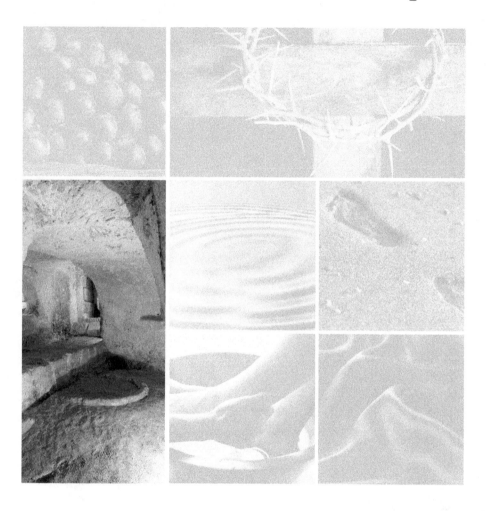

Chapter 2

Meditating
(First Week in Lent)

Meditating

One part of our Lenten journey is to ponder who God is and what God has done. This has been part of the journey of faith for the people of God from the beginning. The psalmist recalls God's mighty deeds for the people of Israel in Psalm 77. Through all the zigs and zags of Israel's history—and the psalmist's own history—there is the recognition that God has been there. God has been present, and God has acted. The psalmist declares: "I will meditate on all your work, and muse on your mighty deeds" (Psalm 77:12).

The time of Lent gives us opportunities to explore deeper dimensions to our faith. We can give attention to what God has been doing. We meditate on the Word of God in Scripture, through which we encounter who God is and the ways God has acted in this world. We meditate on our faith, what we believe. We reflect on our lives and the ways faith affects our lives in many ways, every day.

We realize, in faith, that God is with us and God sees us through the various difficulties of faith we encounter. Our proneness to idolatry, to temptation, and to all the dangers and snares we encounter are met by the continuing "mighty deeds" of God. This God meets us in Jesus Christ, sustains us, guides us, and by grace brings us to where God wants us to be. As we meditate on the nature of faith, we will also experience the comforts and joys of faith, even as we endure whatever comes our way.

In Lent, we can meditate on all God's work. We can see God's "mighty deeds" in acts and events both great and small. We can have a sense of God's guidance for our lives. Our faith is deepened by this meditation. We will find what the Psalmist also found: "You are the God who works wonders" (Psalm 77:14).

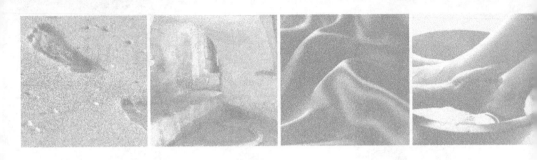

First Sunday in Lent

The Lord brought us out of Egypt with a mighty hand and an outstretched arm, with a terrifying display of power, and with signs and wonders.

Deuteronomy 26:8

Pray
O God, as you act in history, act in our lives that we might do your will. Amen.

Read
Deuteronomy 26:1–11

Reflect
Biblical faith is, above all, faith in a God who reveals himself through historical events, a God who saves in history.

—Gustavo Gutiérrez[5]

Consider
"The God Who Acts" (p. 17)

Action Step
Reflect on times when God has "saved" you.

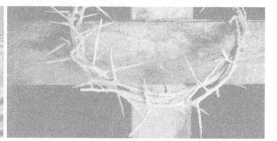

The God Who Acts

The center of the Old Testament is the Exodus event. The Lord God liberated the covenant people, Israel, from their slavery in Egypt. Again and again, the Old Testament looks back to this stupendous event in which the God of Israel acted with a "mighty hand and an outstretched arm" to bring the people out of bondage and into a promised land.

Gustavo Gutiérrez reminds us that the God we find in Scripture is a God who acts in history. We know who God is by what God has done. What God has done is to be involved in human history on behalf of the people of God, doing for them—and for us!—what we cannot do for ourselves. God saves us; and God saves us by what God carries out in the events of our lives.

In Lent, as we meditate on the central event of the New Testament, the death of Jesus Christ, we find ourselves on a Lenten journey that, like the experience of Israel of old, is a journey of twists and turns, of faithfulness and unfaithfulness. We walk each step by faith, sometimes following obediently; sometimes drifting into paths of waywardness in which we turn away from God's will and purposes. But at the foundation of our faith is the conviction God is with us; and that God

> **We find ourselves on a Lenten journey that, like the experience of Israel of old, is a journey of twists and turns, of faithfulness and unfaithfulness.**

acts for us, in the lives we live, every day. We trust God to lead us. We believe that God has acted; and God continues to act in the events of our lives.

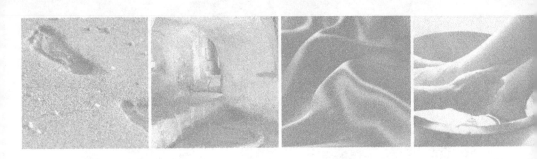

Monday

"And this is eternal life, that they may know you, the only true God, and Jesus Christ whom you have sent."

John 17:3

Pray

O God, help us to know you. In knowing you, may we love you, serve you, and be your faithful people. Amen.

Read

John 17:1–5

Reflect

Minister: What is the chief end of human life?
Child: To know God.

—Calvin's Catechism[6]

Consider

"Our Purpose in Life" (p. 19)

Action Step

Think of ways you would describe your purpose in life. In what ways do these express themselves in your everyday actions?

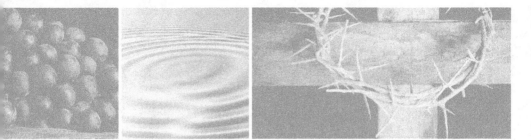

Our Purpose in Life

What's life all about? Is there a purpose to life? Is life worth living? These are the big questions for life. They are the ones that shape our thoughts, desires, and choices.

In 1541 John Calvin wrote a catechism for instructing the children of Geneva who were ten to fifteen years of age. He wanted them to know and understand the Christian faith. Where better to begin that with the basic question of what is the chief end, or purpose, of human life? No other question could say more about what Christians believe and have greater implications for how we are to live.

The child's answer to the minister is simple: "To know God." It is a simple response but with a world of effects. Our life's aim is to know God, even as Jesus himself said in his prayer for his disciples, preceding his death: eternal life is to "know you, the only true God, and Jesus Christ, whom you have sent." All else in life is secondary. Primary is to have a relationship with God and to know in a real and life-changing way who God is and what God has done.

> **Eternal life is to "know you, the only true God, and Jesus Christ, whom you have sent."**

Calvin suggested that to know God is to honor God, to rely on God, to obey God, to call on God, to seek salvation in God, and to acknowledge that all our good comes from God. This is our purpose in life.

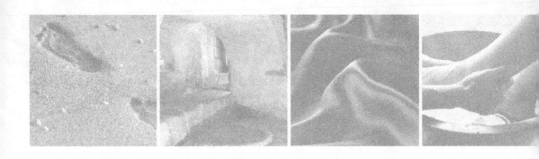

Tuesday

Commit your way to the LORD; trust in him, and he will act.

Psalm 37:5

Pray
O God, our hearts are restless until they find their rest in thee. May our hearts rest in you, by faith. Amen.

Read
Psalm 37:1–7

Reflect
Faith is the resting of the heart on God, the author of life and eternal salvation, so that we may be saved from all evil through him and may follow all good.

—William Ames[7]

Consider
"Faith" (p. 21)

Action Step
Describe ways in which your faith engages your mind, comforts your heart, and engages your hands in actions.

Faith

Mark Twain described a schoolboy's definition as "Faith is believing what you know ain't so." Many people believe this definition and live as if it *is* so.

The Psalmist had a better view. It was grounded in what God has done. Faith engages not just our minds, but also our hearts and hands. Faith means trust. Faith is entrusting one's self. Faith is committing your way in life to God, trusting in God, and experiencing that God acts. This is not detached intellectualism. It is not an endless wrangling about ideas—theoretical discussions about God's existence or reality. It is a full involvement of the self, a participation in the life of God, whom we Christians know in Jesus Christ. Our knowledge of God is a life lived *in* God.

Our knowledge of God is a life lived *in* God.

William Ames, who wrote theological volumes about God, captured the basic nature of faith when he saw it as a "resting of the heart on God." God has given us life and salvation, saving us from evil. This God acts. Faith enables us to follow God's way, as the way of "all good." Faith is entrusting ourselves, resting our hearts on God, and committing ourselves to following God's way, in Jesus Christ. Faith fills our lives with fullness!

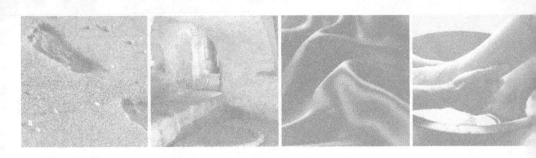

Wednesday

"You shall not make for yourself an idol."

Exodus 20:4

Pray
O God, be at the center of our lives. Help us to love you more than all else. Help us to serve you with our whole selves. Amen.

Read
Exodus 20:1–21

Reflect
Idolatry is the practice of ascribing absolute value to things of relative worth.

—Frederick Buechner[8]

Consider
"Idolatry" (p. 23)

Action Step
Ponder this question: What are idols in your life? Think of ways these may be overcome and ways your priorities can shift so God will be valued above all.

Idolatry

Did you ever notice that the Bible doesn't spend any time arguing for the existence of God? Open the first page of Scripture and you'll find that "In the beginning, God created the heavens and the earth" (Genesis 1:1; RSV). No intellectual arguments based on reason are invoked to describe what happened. God was there, and God began to create. Case closed. The basic reality in the universe is the God who created the universe.

What the Bible is much more concerned about than the existence of God is what humans do in relation to this God. Do we obey God, love God, and serve God? Or are there other agendas for our lives? What do we love? What do we value?

The Ten Commandments prohibit idolatry. In Israel's context, it was forbidden to make an idol, in any form. Idols should not be bowed down to, or worshiped. But physical idols are not all that is covered.

Frederick Buechner defines idolatry as giving absolute value to things of only relative worth. When we put any person or thing in the place of God—the one who has absolute value in our lives—we construct an idol. When we love and value things that can be good in themselves, but put so much of ourselves into them that they take on a central place in our lives, we construct idols. To do an "idol check" in our lives we need to ask ourselves about where we are putting our energies, where we are investing our wealth, where our values lie, and to where our affections are turned. Lent is the time to do this. Only God is ultimate, the One to love and value above all.

> **We need to ask ourselves about where we are putting our energies, where we are investing our wealth, where our values lie, and to where our affections are turned.**

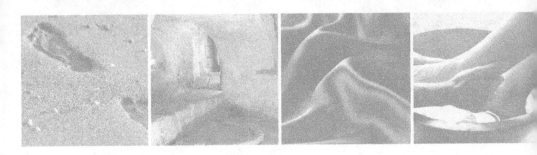

Thursday

Then Jesus was led up by the Spirit into the wilderness to be tempted by the devil.

Matthew 4:1

Pray
May we recognize temptations, O God, resist them; and resolve to live faithfully according to your Word. Amen.

Read
Matthew 4:1–11

Reflect
Temptation is entanglement with anything *that subdues, chokes, misfires, or distorts our holy desire.*

—*Wendy Farley*[9]

Consider
"Temptation" (p. 25)

Action Step
List the temptations in your life that subdue your desire for God. Write a way to subdue each temptation.

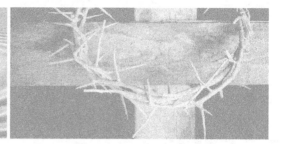

Temptation

Temptations come to us in lots of ways. Some are very clear: Do I slip this store merchandise into my pocket? Do I fudge some numbers on my taxes? Do I turn away when I see someone in need? Other times temptations are subtler: Do I seek my own advancement, even if it will harm others? Do I let myself drift away from the church and let my faith droop by neglecting prayer and Bible reading?

Jesus faced temptations head-on in his experience in the wilderness. He rejected the devil's allurements of seeking power and testing God. He also resisted the urge to turn stones to bread—which was especially tough, since Jesus was "famished" (Matthew 4:2). Being fed is good in itself, but not when it comes with the price of dealing with the devil!

Wendy Farley helps us understand temptation by seeing it as an entanglement that turns us away from holy desire. We can understand holy desire as loving God, serving God, and living in the relationships God intends. When that desire is subdued, or choked, or fails, or is distorted, and we are caught in it all, temptation is real, and we may give in. This can all happen easily, in the midst of good choices we make, every day. So our need is always to keep watch, to look within ourselves, to see the help of those in the church or of others who are also special to us, to keep our lives focused on the holy desires that should be at the core of who we are.

> **Wendy Farley helps us understand temptation by seeing it as an entanglement that turns us away from holy desire.**

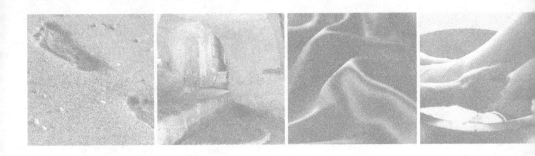

Friday

But God, who is rich in mercy . . . made us alive together with Christ.

Ephesians 2:4, 5

Pray
God, you are rich in mercy. Be merciful to me. May I recognize expressions of your grace in all the different parts of my life. Amen.

Read
Ephesians 2:1–10

Reflect
This is the main purpose of the Gospel, that, although we are by nature children of wrath, the quarrel between God and us can be resolved and He can receive us into His grace.

—John Calvin[10]

Consider
"The Purpose of the Gospel" (p. 27)

Action Step
Reflect on ways in which the grace of God is real to you. Share one of these ways with a friend or family member.

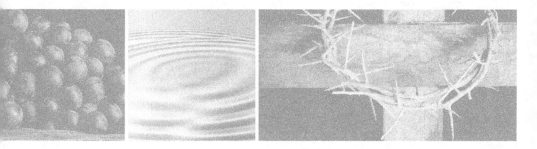

The Purpose of the Gospel

In Lent, we look inwardly, reflecting on who we are, what we do, and to what God is calling us in Jesus Christ. We also reflect on the gospel of Jesus Christ that forms our identity as members of the church and followers of Jesus.

The story is the same for all of us, even with every variation imaginable. We are "dead through our trespasses" (Ephesians 2:5), cut off from God by choosing to live life "our way," instead of God's way. So dreadful is our sinfulness that we are cut off from God and called "children of wrath."

But the good news of the gospel—and the purpose of the gospel, according to John Calvin—is that our "quarrel" with God can be resolved. Our hostilities can be ended; we can be received into the grace of God, through Jesus Christ—who has died to make our reconciliation possible. As we hear when we confess our sin in church: "In Jesus Christ, we are forgiven!"

> **Our "quarrel" with God can be resolved.**

We are "alive together with Christ." What more wonderful purpose of the gospel can we imagine? To receive the gift of the grace of God, to become "alive," to be given new life—all of this is from God's great love and mercy. God gives us the gift of faith to receive the grace that makes "all things new" (Revelation 21:5).

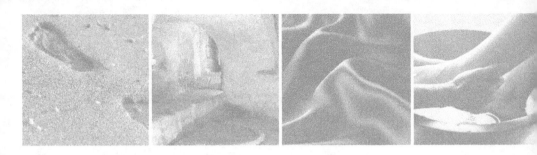

Saturday

Who will separate us from the love of Christ?

Romans 8:35

Pray

O triune God—Father, Son, and Holy Spirit—hold us in your hands, protect us, and comfort us, always. Amen.

Read

Romans 8:31–39

Reflect

In life and in death we belong to God.
Through the grace of our Lord Jesus Christ,
the love of God,
and the communion of the Holy Spirit . . . .

—A Brief Statement of Faith[11]

Consider

"The Comfort of Faith" (p. 29)

Action Step

Consider the differences between a comfort based on "hoping for the best" compared with the comfort of faith grounded in the actions of God. Write a prayer thanking God for your comfort.

The Comfort of Faith

We all need to belong. It is one of our basic urges. We want to feel as though we are not isolated, left on our own, doomed to face life playing solitaire. Social creatures that we are, we need a sense of participation in something bigger than ourselves, in a group that may care for us. Most of all, in a personal sense, we seek assurance and security that we are connected with others—and, even, with God.

The apostle Paul's ringing affirmation in Romans 8 that we belong to God in Jesus Christ is the heart of what we need. No words can affect us more deeply. God is for us, God justifies us, Jesus Christ died for us and intercedes for us with God. This is not a temporary condition. This is our union with Christ by faith that lasts eternally. What's more, nothing—in all creation—can separate us from "the love of God in Christ Jesus our Lord" (Romans 8:39).

A Brief Statement of Faith captures this in its opening lines, affirming our belonging to God in life and in death. Our belonging by faith in the here and now carries over into eternity, after our physical death. The words of assurance are grounded in the actions of God for us: the grace of Jesus Christ, the love of God, the communion of the Holy Spirit. This is the comfort of faith that nothing can take away.

We seek assurance and security that we are connected with others—and, even, with God.

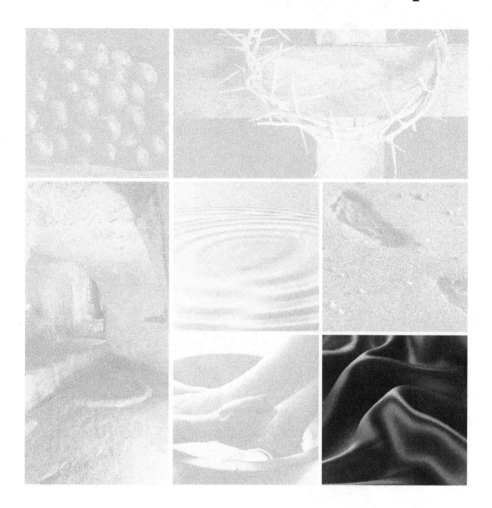

Chapter 3

Praying
(Second Week in Lent)

Praying

One of the central practices of Christian faith is prayer. We practice prayer in many ways, recognizing that it is our true lifeline with God. During Lent, our prayer lives can be strengthened. We can be more deliberate in our praying—in the time we take to pray, in the focus of our prayers, in our sense of God's presence as we participate in prayer with the triune God.

Prayer is conversation with God. It is a true expression of who we are, of what we are thinking and feeling. In prayer, we "let it all hang out" before the One who calls us to prayer and invites us to pray in such a way that prayer becomes as natural to us as breathing.

Yet, at times, prayer can be hard work. When so much wells up within us, when so many conflicting thoughts and feelings swirl around us, it can seem that our prayers are all a jumble, with no pattern or coherence to them. But we need not fear. One of the deepest joys of prayer is to realize the Holy Spirit "helps us in our weakness; for we do not know how to pray as we ought, but that very Spirit intercedes with sighs too deep for words" (Romans 8:26). The Spirit sorts it all out. Even more, the Spirit presents our prayers to God with a deep striving, interceding for us, and God "knows what is in the mind of the Spirit" (Romans 8:27). This is our true comfort in prayer. Our prayers do not need to be perfect. The Spirit takes our prayers and presents them to God, just as Jesus Christ intercedes for us (Romans 8:34). In prayer, the whole Trinity is involved in our prayers, right along with us!

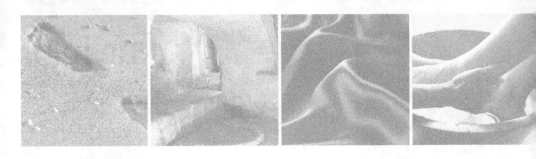

Second Sunday in Lent

Hear, O LORD, when I cry aloud, be gracious to me and answer me!

Psalm 27:7

Pray
Hear our prayers and answer us according to your grace, O God. Hear our prayers to do your will. Amen.

Read
Psalm 27

Reflect
The purpose of the prayer of petition is not to have our own way but to bring our will into conformity with the will of God.

—Donald G. Bloesch[12]

Consider
"When I Cry Aloud" (p. 35)

Action Step
Think of the recent prayers you have offered to God. See if your requests to God are primarily focused on getting your own way, or on living in God's way.

When I Cry Aloud

In Lent, we seek to pray more often and take prayer more seriously. We recognize prayer as a means of God's grace to us, as a way by which through conversation with God, we find God's will and directions for our lives. Our various types of prayer— adoration and praise, confession, petition and supplication, thanksgiving—all are ways we express ourselves to God and listen for ways God communicates to us.

The Psalmist knew that God heard prayers offered to the Lord. Prayers can be cried aloud, as an expression of the depths of our feelings as we pray. The Psalmist sought God to be gracious and to answer his prayers. He could pray this way, confident that God is a gracious God and that God does answer the prayers of God's people. Yet even when our faith may sputter, we can believe that God continues to be who God is and does what God will do.

Donald Bloesch helps us recognize that when we pray to God with petitions—with what we ask of God—our purpose should not be to get our own way, to dictate to God what *we* want. Our prayers of petition should be to bring our wills into accordance with God's will for us. We want, above all else, to be and to do what God desires. When we cry aloud, we lay out our petitions before God, trusting God to be gracious and to answer us. But our greatest request is that what we pray for will unite us with the will of God.

> **Our prayers of petition should be to bring our wills into accordance with God's will for us.**

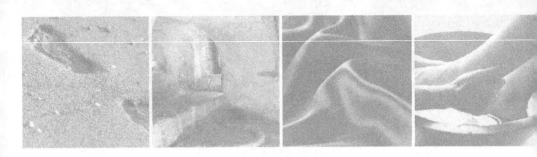

Monday

Rejoice always, pray without ceasing.

1 Thessalonians 5:17

Pray

Life is all one piece, O God. Help us have a consciousness of you always present. Help us live, thinking and praying about what you want us to be and do. Amen.

Read

1 Thessalonians 5:12–22

Reflect

Pray without ceasing in this sense. Pray without a break between your prayer and your life. Pray so that there is a real continuity between your prayer and your whole actual life.

—*P. T. Forsyth*[13]

Consider

"Pray without Ceasing" (p. 37)

Action Step

Make a conscious effort to offer prayers as you go through a day. See ways that what you do relates to the prayers you offer.

Pray without Ceasing

Some instructions in the Bible seem nearly impossible to fulfill, such as "Be perfect, therefore, as your heavenly Father is perfect" (Matthew 5:48), "Be at peace with one another" (Mark 9:50b), and "Pray without ceasing" (1 Thessalonians 5:17).

Our prayer life is often pretty much set apart from the rest of life. When we take time to pray, we do it in a quiet place, with no distractions, hoping our thoughts and words don't bounce off the ceiling and come back down to earth. We hope God hears—and answers—our prayers.

But how can we "pray without ceasing," as Paul urges the Thessalonians? We live busy lives. We may not even take much time out to pray. So how do we understand Paul's words?

How can we "pray without ceasing"?

P. T. Forsyth helps us with this by urging us to see that prayer and life are intimately connected. Our whole lives should be, in some sense, a prayer. Prayers are offered to God as expressions of our trust, obedience, and love. So we should seek continuity, mutuality between our lives and our prayers, our prayers and our lives. There is not our "prayer life" and our "other life." They are one. As we live, we can offer prayers—anytime, for anything. We should make prayer as natural to us as breathing, so that as we breathe, we pray. As we pray, we live.

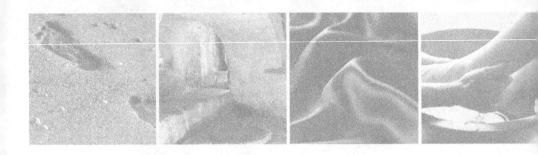

Tuesday

"Could you not stay awake with me one hour? Stay awake and pray."

Matthew 26:40, 41

Pray
Keep us awake and praying, O Lord—awake to see what you are doing in this world, and praying, always, to know your will and to do it. Amen.

Read
Matthew 26:36–46

Reflect
What else is Christian spirituality except watching and praying, watching prayerfully and praying watchfully?

—Jürgen Moltmann[14]

Consider
"Praying and Watching" (p. 39)

Action Step
Look at ways in which the pattern of watching and praying/praying and watching takes shape in your life. Be more aware of both aspects.

Praying and Watching

There is always a great sadness in the story of Jesus' prayer in Gethsemane. His inner circles of disciples were with him, and he asked them to stay awake with him. But the disciples fall asleep. In the midst of his agony upon his impending death, Jesus' closest friends could not "watch" with him, stay awake to support him in the midst of his great anguish.

Staying awake and being watchful was something Jesus urged (Mark 13:33), as did the apostle Paul (1 Thessalonians 5:6). In the Garden of Gethsemane, this alertness is connected with Jesus' prayer.

This led Jürgen Moltmann to see a whole pattern of Christian spirituality, or Christian living. We are to "watch prayerfully" and "pray watchfully." This is a rhythm of the Christian life, a pattern we can adopt in Lent and beyond.

We watch prayerfully. As we look at the world, its people, our church, family, and others we love, we are aware of their needs and hopes. We watch their lives and pray for their lives. We connect with others, in love, when we pray for them and for all that means much to them.

> **We connect with others, in love, when we pray for them and for all that means much to them.**

We pray watchfully. As we pray, we watch for what God is doing in the world, in the church, and in our lives and the lives of those we love. The excitement of the Christian life is seeing ways in which God answers our prayers; and even more, seeing what God is doing in the world. In this sense, we should pray with our eyes wide open!

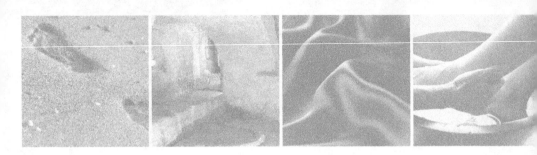

Wednesday

"We, for our part, will devote ourselves to prayer and to serving the word."

Acts 6:4

Pray
Help us to see our work as forms of prayer, dear God. Help us to know what you are calling us to do, when we pray. Amen.

Read
Acts 6:1–6

Reflect
The practice of Christian prayer, however, cannot be separated from service and work for God's reign. Praying is always to be accompanied by working. Christians do not pray rather than work, or work rather than pray. The practice of Christian hope requires both. Prayer inspires service, and service always begins and ends in prayer.

—Daniel L. Migliore[15]

Consider
"Praying and Working" (p. 41)

Action Step
Consider ways in which your own actions can become a part of your prayers. Ask God to show you what actions to do.

Praying and Working

The days of the earliest church were yeasty times. As we see in the book of Acts, early Christians were active, engaged and finding their way to doing what needed to be done as a community: worshiping, teaching, praying, and taking care of basic needs for food and all else (Acts 4:34).

As Daniel Migliore points out, prayer goes hand in hand with service and work for the reign of God. While early Christians prayed fervently, they also worked fervently. They did the things that needed to be done, on behalf of others, and for the sake of the Lord Jesus Christ. They could rely on God in prayer— thanking and petitioning God. But they saw that their prayers led them to serving others. They did not sit back and "let God do it." Their prayer led to service, and the ways they met the needs of others began and ended with prayer.

Their prayer led to service, and the ways they met the needs of others began and ended with prayer.

Our prayers should lead us in the same directions. Praying and working are two sides of the same coin. All we try to do as members of the church, in ministry, is but a small step toward the new world God will bring. But it is a step, just the same. Praying and working is the rhythm of our lives.

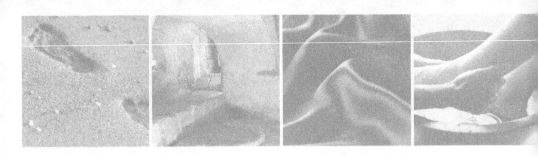

Thursday

Trust in him at all times, O people; pour out your heart before him; God is a refuge for us.

Psalm 62:8

Pray
Hear our prayers for others, O God. Amen.

Read
Psalm 62

Reflect
We pray for particular people and situations in order to place ourselves in God's hand, and live out these ways in our own lives. In interceding for others, we place ourselves attentively in the presence of God so that God might use us for the transformation of the world.

—Martha Moore-Keish[16]

Consider
"Praying for Others" (p. 43)

Action Step
Make a list of the people for whom you pray, or list those for whom you want to pray. Commit yourself to praying for these people daily.

Praying for Others

One of the great gifts we've been given is the opportunity to pray for other people. We pray for ourselves. But beyond that, our prayers for others entrust them and their lives to the gracious provision of God. We pray for others not only because we know that God wants us to do so (James 5:16) but also as a way of showing our love and care for those whose needs we know.

We believe that God hears and answers our prayers for others. We trust God to hear and act at all times and we trust that we can pour out our hearts before God, reflecting the words of the Psalmist. Without this faith and confidence that God can be trusted and God can help, our prayers would have no effect and would be of no use to make. But God is a "refuge for us," and to believe that about God means we can have hope in believing that God's power is at work for others.

Martha Moore-Keish tells us that in praying for others and for situations, we entrust ourselves to God's hands. This helps us to recognize God's ways in the world and to live out God's ways in our own lives. As we pray for others, we also give ourselves to God, to be used for God's will and purposes in transforming the world.

In praying for others and for situations, we entrust ourselves to God's hands.

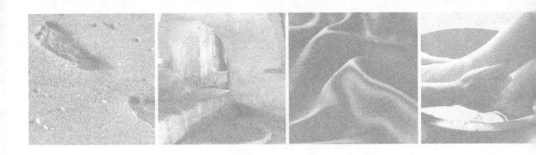

Friday

I urge that supplications, prayers, intercessions, and thanksgivings be made for everyone.

1 Timothy 2:1

Pray
Loving God, help us to be loving toward others and to overcome difficult relationships through prayer. Amen.

Read
1 Timothy 2:1–4

Reflect
No one can feel hatred towards those for whom he prays.

—John Chrysostom[17]

Consider
"No Hatred When We Pray" (p. 45)

Action Step
Think of those with whom you have had or have difficult relationships. Pray for them.

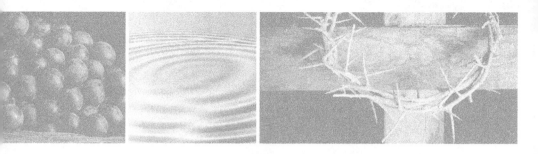

No Hatred When We Pray

Our call to pray for everyone is clear in the Scriptures. In the instructions in 1 Timothy, the writer urges all manner of prayers: supplications, intercessions, and thanksgiving "for everyone." There are no exceptions. The instructions go on to indicate the writer's desire that the prayers be offered "without anger or argument" (1 Timothy 2:8).

We often need to hear this message. It is easy to be restrictive in our prayers. We pray only for those people or situations that are near and dear to our hearts. This is good and important. But we shouldn't stop there. We should go on to enlarge our circle of prayer so that a wider group is included. The wider group should widen far enough to include the whole world.

Jesus even commanded us to love our enemies and to "pray for those who persecute you" (Matthew 5:44). This surely enlarges our circle for prayer! Imagine, praying for those who "despitefully use" you (KJV).

These commands point us to an insight from the early church theologian John Chrysostom, who said that we cannot feel hatred for those for whom we pray. When we pray for others, even those who harm us, our hatreds melt away. Our anger is abated. Prayer, in the presence of God, affects not only those for whom we pray; it affects us as well. Prayer can help our hatreds to subside and for us to be enabled to offer supplications,

When we pray for others, even those who harm us, our hatreds melt away.

intercessions, and thanksgiving, even for those who have done us wrong. There is a miraculous power in prayer. As we pray for all others, their lives and our lives can be changed.

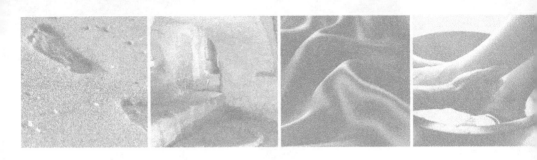

Saturday

And will not God grant justice to his chosen ones who cry to him day and night? . . . I tell you, he will quickly grant justice to them.

Luke 18:7, 8

Pray
O God of justice, give us eyes to see injustices and give us the will to pray and to work against injustices. Amen.

Read
Luke 18:1–8

Reflect
Praying and crying to God against injustices describes the whole life of the believers: their efforts, their protests against injustice. It describes also their trust in God, for they know that God acts very differently than the unjust judge.

—*Luise Schottroff*[18]

Consider
"Praying Against Injustices" (p. 47)

Action Step
Identify injustices of which you are aware. Pray for God's help against them. Involve yourself in working to right them.

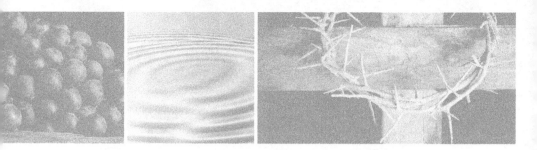

Praying Against Injustices

Sometimes the contrasts between God and humans are the greatest imaginable. We as humans are limited and finite. God is unlimited and infinite. We humans are sinners; God is perfect and holy. We humans are unjust; God is just.

This was the point of Jesus' parable about the unjust judge. The widow had to keep complaining, seeking justice from a judge who had "no fear of God and no respect for anyone" (Luke 18:4). But the judge relented, given the widow's perseverance in "continually coming" to him.

How much more will God, the righteous and just judge, bring justice to those who are oppressed? As Luise Schottroff says, believers need to continue in "praying and crying to God against injustices." These are our attitudes and actions. This is "the whole life of the believers." We pray and cry for justice, trusting in a just God who will act "very differently than the unjust judge" and will help those who pray and cry, granting justice to them.

> **How much more will God, the righteous and just judge, bring justice to those who are oppressed?**

In Lent, it is easy to get so oriented to our interiors, our own situations and spiritual life, that we forget this basic component of Christian living. Christians pray to God for justice for all who are oppressed. We support and work for justice for those whose needs are great. Lent is the time to refocus our efforts in trusting God to act and acting ourselves against injustices.

Chapter 4

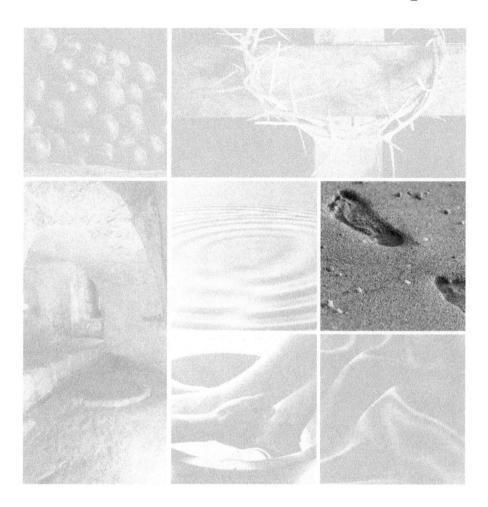

Loving
(Third Week in Lent)

Loving

A popular song for Christian youth some years ago said: "Love, love, love, love. The gospel in a word is love."

We might think this is a simple song. But its truth is profound. The Christian gospel is centered in God's love for the world and the matchless expression of that love in God's Son, Jesus Christ. When we look at Jesus—his life, death, and resurrection—we see God's love in person. We see the kind of people God wants us to be. In Jesus Christ, God-with-us, God's love has come to us, in a person.

Lent is a time for focusing on God's love in Jesus Christ. The love brings salvation, through Christ's death on the cross. This love brings us new life as we are transformed by the power of God's love within us, by the Holy Spirit. This love binds us together in the church, the body of Christ, where a community of love is marked by mutual care, burden bearing, and service to others—in the church and in the world.

The love of God in Christ that captivates leads us to loving others. It leads us to loving enemies, to those who mistreat or betray us. It leads us to directing our lives outwardly, toward sharing God's love in Christ, instead of inwardly where we are concerned primarily with ourselves. This love in Christ gives our lives an extreme makeover, because we now have a new purpose and a new path to follow. Our Lenten journey leads us from Christ into the world in ministering to others, just as God in Christ has ministered to us.

The verse that follows Paul's great chapter on love in 1 Corinthians 13 finds Paul saying simply: "Pursue love" (1 Corinthians 14:1). We pursue love, in all ways—love for enemies, for the church, for all in the world—because God has loved us with a deep and everlasting love in Jesus Christ. In the words of the First Letter of John: "Beloved, since God loved us so much, we also ought to love one another" (1 John 4:11). So we can sing: "Love, love, love, love. The gospel in a word is love"!

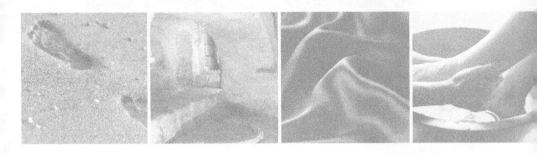

Third Sunday in Lent

*"This son of mine was dead and is alive again; he was lost
and is found!" And they began to celebrate.*

Luke 15:24

Pray
*O God, you love more than we can ever know or realize. May your
love be real to us, no matter where we have been or what we have
done. Amen.*

Read
Luke 15:11–32

Reflect
*A kind Father when thou gavest; and kinder still when he returned
destitute.*

—Augustine[19]

Consider
"God Loves Like That" (p. 53)

Action Step
Reflect on ways you have failed, your sins. Pray and confess. Receive
God's overflowing love that welcomes you home.

God Loves Like That

Jesus' parable of the Prodigal Son captures the heart of God. It tells us of a parent who gives extravagant, undeserved, loving grace to the son who had spent all he had been given and returned home in humiliation and disgrace. Jesus says God loves like that.

Augustine captured the essence of this description of God when he noted that the kind parent gave all the inheritance of the household to the son who wanted to set out on his own. This love let go of a beloved son. But this kindness and love reached an even deeper level when the son returned empty, destitute. As the Scripture says, the father ran to receive him, embraced him, and welcomed him home. The son who had been dead was alive; the one who had been lost was found.

In Lent, this message comes home to us with profound meaning. Our use of our freedom has led to sins and to wanderings so we have drifted far away from the household of God. God honors our choices. But in "coming to ourselves," as the prodigal did (Luke 15:17), we return home to find a God who does not bash us or humiliate us or cast us out. We find a God who loves us because we are now where we should be, in the family home. The heart of God reaches out to us in love. It is a love that embraces us, even after all our misdeeds, after our neglect and less than faithful obedience. No wonder the household can celebrate. God loves like that!

> **We find a God who loves us because we are now where we should be, in the family home.**

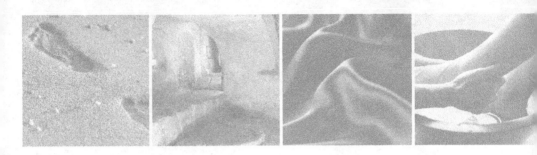

Monday

And live in love, as Christ loved us and gave himself up for us.

Ephesians 5:2

Pray
Dear Jesus, you have given us a pattern to follow in our lives. Help us to follow and especially help us to show love. Amen.

Read
Ephesians 5:1–2

Reflect
As children of God, we are born with a purpose in creation and need to carry out our purpose, which involves living a life similar to that of Jesus Christ.

—Grace Ji-Sun Kim[20]

Consider
"Carrying Out Our Purpose" (p. 55)

Action Step
Reflect on the life of Jesus and the kinds of acts he did that you need to follow. Then put these into practice.

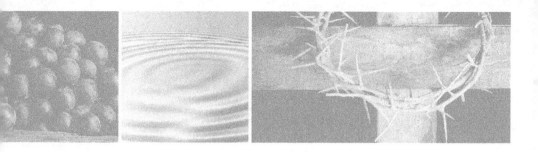

Carrying Out Our Purpose

Living into Lent means following Jesus Christ as our Lord and Savior. What that means in the church for all its members varies with all the callings and gifts we have been given.

But one thing is the same for us all. We are disciples of Jesus Christ who follow Jesus best by living the way he showed us. This is what God desires and what Jesus expects of those who name his name.

Grace Ji-Sun Kim points to this when she writes that God's children have a purpose. This purpose is rooted in God's creation of each of us. We carry out our purpose, as Christians, by living our lives in accord with how Jesus lived his.

Our Scripture tells us that Jesus lived his life in love. He loved us and died for us, giving himself on our behalf. Love characterized Jesus' life and is to be the primary motive in ours. God's purpose in creating us is for us to live out God's love, seen most fully in Jesus Christ.

Is love the dominant direction we pursue? Do we love those who do not love us, who misuse us, who work against us? The self-giving love of Jesus is the love we are created to share. We follow the life Jesus showed us. This means love is at the center.

> **We carry out our purpose, as Christians, by living our lives in accord with how Jesus lived his.**

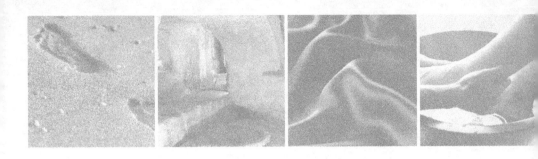

Tuesday

"For God so loved the world that he gave his only Son, so that everyone who believes in him may not perish but may have eternal life."

John 3:16

Pray
Open our eyes and hearts to those who need your love, O God who has loved us all. Amen.

Read
John 3:16–21

Reflect
The expansive scope of God's love in Jesus Christ means that all are invited, all are included.

—Kendra G. Hotz[21]

Consider
"God's Love Is for All" (p. 57)

Action Step
Think of people whose lives need the power of love. Do what you can to put love into action for them.

God's Love Is for All

Did you ever notice that more you get involved in church, in mission and ministry, the wider the range of your love becomes? It always happens. When you take on a new direction, becoming involved in what the church is doing in the lives of others, giving of yourself so the love and justice and peace of Jesus Christ can be enacted in new and significant ways, you find more people to love. You find more people included in those for whom you pray and whose lives become important to you.

We should expect this, shouldn't we? As the most famous verse in the Bible tells us: God loved the world so much that God sent Jesus Christ to die for us; so those who believe in him will not be lost, but have life eternal. Martin Luther called John 3:16 the gospel in a nutshell.

The gospel is the good news of God's love. As Kendra Hotz puts it, God's love is expansive, continuing to invite all to receive God's love, and including all people to be recipients of God's love.

> **God's love is expansive, continuing to invite all to receive God's love, and including all people to be recipients of God's love.**

In Jesus Christ God has reached out and hugged the world, bringing the whole human family into the family of which we are a part. God's love is for all. Those who believe in Jesus Christ experience God's great love, embracing us.

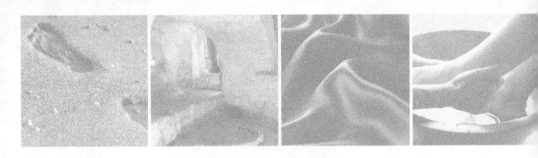

Wednesday

The only thing that counts is faith working through love.

Galatians 5:6

Pray
You grant us the gift of faith, O God; help us to receive faith gladly.
You grant us love to share with others; help us to share love gladly.
Amen.

Read
Galatians 5:2–6

Reflect
Faith is a hand to take hold on Christ and his benefits. Love is a hand to give out tokens of faith both to God and to man.

—William Perkins[22]

Consider
"Faith and Love" (p. 59)

Action Step
Reflect on ways your faith and love go together. List ways your faith can be strengthened. List ways you can live out love more fully.

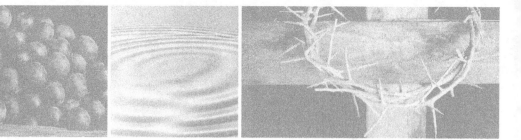

Faith and Love

Faith and love are much on our minds during Lent. Our faith is directed to who Jesus Christ is and what he does for our salvation, bringing us new, eternal life. In love we live out our salvation and express—with our love—the love we have been given in Christ.

Living in Christian discipleship, we find faith and love together at every turn. The apostle Paul described the nature of the Christian life as being "faith working through love." This is "the only thing that counts" for Paul. In a real sense, this is the truest expression of who we are as Christian people: we live by faith and express that faith through love.

This is the truest expression of who we are as Christian people: we live by faith and express that faith through love.

William Perkins put it in terms of two hands. By faith, we take hold of Christ and his benefits—that is, what Christ has done for us in living, dying, and being raised again for our salvation. Faith is one hand. The other hand is the hand of love by which we give out "tokens of faith," said Perkins, both to God and to others.

As we live our faith, we express that faith to others by loving them with the same love we have for God, and which God has shown for us in Jesus Christ. The two hands work together. One without the other is incomplete. Both together express the fullness of the gospel.

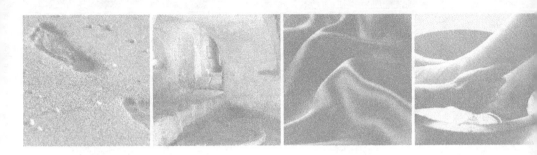

Thursday

I give you a new commandment, that you love one another. Just as I have loved you, you also should love one another.

John 13:34

Pray
Sometimes it is hard to love others, O Christ. Make your love alive in us and help us love one another. Amen.

Read
John 13:31–35

Reflect
For this very end, therefore, did He love us, that we also should love one another; bestowing this on us by His own love to us, that we should be bound to one another in mutual love, and united together as members by so pleasant a bond, should be the body of so mighty a Head.

—Augustine[23]

Consider
"Love One Another" (p. 61)

Action Step
Consider ways to enlarge the circle of those for whom you can act in love. List and do practical things to convey love to them.

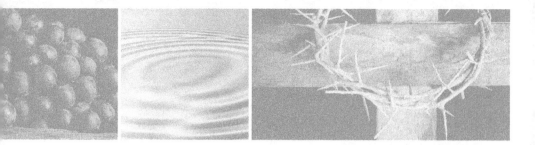

Love One Another

A well-known saying about the early church came from those in Roman society who said of the Christians: See how they love one another.

In this, the Christians were carrying out the command of Jesus when he established love as the central mark of discipleship and instructed his disciples to love one another. He used himself as the example. The many expressions of Jesus' love for his followers showed those of his company not only what the nature of love is but also that the love Jesus had for them was to be expressed in their lives as love for others.

Augustine interpreted this command as meaning that the love Christ gives to his followers binds us to one another and unites us in the body of Christ. Christ is our head. It is to him we look. As we do, we will see the most amazing love, a love that even went to death on a cross to show God's love to the world.

> **The love Christ gives to his followers binds us to one another and unites us in the body of Christ.**

We love one another in the church but we also go on to love others in the world—the same world for whom Jesus Christ came to die. Our love spreads. We are bound together in Christ's love in the church, and we share that love with those who need to experience being loved.

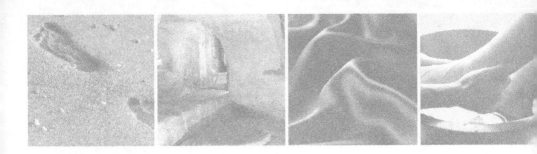

Friday

A poor widow came and put in two small copper coins, which are worth a penny.

Mark 12:42

Pray
We give you but your own, dear Lord. We give you our lives to be used in sharing ourselves with others. Amen.

Read
Mark 12:41–44

Reflect
If we become those two small copper coins, we must live our lives in such a way that our offering is truly shared with others.

—Emilie M. Townes[24]

Consider
"Sharing Ourselves with Others" (p. 63)

Action Step
Find new ways to share your life with others—in the church, in the community.

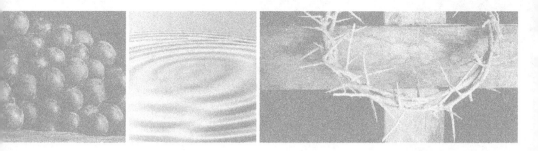

Sharing Ourselves with Others

Some of us may have grown up hearing this story of the widow depositing two coins into the temple offering as the story of the "widow's mite." A "mite" was not a coin found in Israel during the time of Jesus. It was found in England in the seventeenth century, when the King James Version was translated. In this version, the widow "threw in two mites" (KJV).

The point was that the widow contributed the least valuable coins available. But she gave all she had. It was not the amount of the gift, but the fact that "she out of her poverty has put in everything she had, all she had to live on" (Mark 12:44) that drew praise from Jesus.

The widow shared out of her poverty. As Emilie Townes imagines, we can become those two small copper coins as we offer ourselves to God in Christ. When we do, the offering of ourselves obliges us to live in a way in which we truly share ourselves with others. Giving our whole selves to Christ puts us into circulation with others, in the church and in the world. We care for and love and serve others as we give ourselves to them. We find ways to live "for others," because we have given our whole selves to be disciples of Jesus Christ.

> **We can become those two small copper coins as we offer ourselves to God in Christ.**

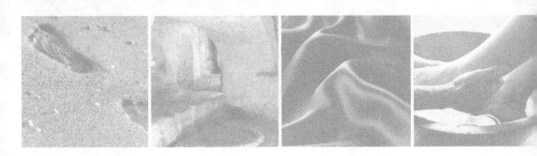

Saturday

I was hungry and you gave me food, I was thirsty and you gave me something to drink, I was a stranger and you welcomed me.

Matthew 25:35

Pray
O Lord Jesus Christ, you meet us in the faces of those in need. May we respond to them with help, knowing that we are also responding to you. Amen.

Read
Matthew 25:31–46

Reflect
Now there is no greater service of God than Christian love which helps and serves the needy, as Christ himself will judge and testify at the Last Day.

—Martin Luther[25]

Consider
"Serving the Needy" (p. 65)

Action Step
Examine the human needs around you. Make it part of your life to try to alleviate these needs in whatever ways possible.

Serving the Needy

There is only one parable of Jesus where he refers to himself as a judge. In the Judgment of the Nations parable, people all stand before the Son of Man. The result is judgment or blessedness.

In this parable, what is central is what one has done in life. Have we responded to human need? Have we met the needs of others for food, drink, clothing; have we visited the sick, the imprisoned? Have we welcomed the stranger? Our actions either express our love as disciples of Jesus Christ or not.

Have we reached out in love and service to those in need?

Martin Luther said there is "no greater service of God" than this Christian love that reaches out to help and serve the needy. This serving the needy is not an option for the Christian life. It is an absolute necessity. It is a standard to which we are held. Have we reached out in love and service to those in need? For Luther, the ultimate importance of this is that "Christ himself" will judge on these things at the Last Day.

There is no better time than Lent to get this priority of the Christian life into focus. Finding ways to live out genuine service to those in need is a matter of spiritual well-being. Serving the needy is big in the heart of Jesus, as he himself served those in need throughout his ministry.

Chapter 5

Thanking
(Fourth Week in Lent)

Thanking

Someone said we should have pity for atheists because they have no one to whom to give thanks!

Christians are thankful people. Each year in November, we often sing the hymn "Come, Ye Thankful People, Come." We have a national day of Thanksgiving in the United States. Thankfulness forms the core of our Christian lives, in every season, every day.

Our giving thanks to God is our response. It is our response to all God has done for the world and for us. Gratitude is the essential center of our faith. It is the heartbeat from which all flows. When we consider the whole story of God's great and wondrous acts conveyed to us in Scripture, we are overwhelmed with great gratitude. We spend our lives thanking God for being who God is and for doing for us what we could never do for ourselves.

Our thanking God takes many forms. Certainly, we praise God, as we come together in the church community. Our great hymns of the faith lift us beyond our own words and into the words of the whole Christian community. We are united in praise to the God who has called us, blessed us, and given us the gift of salvation in Jesus Christ.

We praise God in prayer, as we participate in God's gracious invitation to have conversation with God. From our praise arise our petitions, laying before God our needs and hopes. We thank God for hearing our prayers, assured that what we pray is heard by the One who is the source of all our blessings.

Most fully, we thank God by living lives of gratitude. All we say and do as followers of Jesus Christ emerges from the depths of thanksgiving to this God who loves us in Christ. We are people not only of "thanksgiving," but also of "thanksliving." Our lives of gratitude are expressions of the grace we have been given.

Our Lenten journeys are steps of praise and thanks. We look always to the God who loves us in Jesus Christ. With Paul, we say, "Thanks be to God, who in Christ always leads us" (2 Corinthians 2:14).

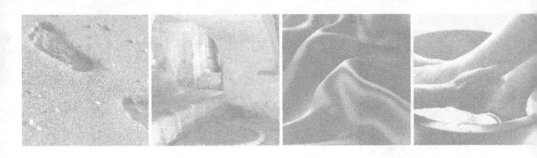

Fourth Sunday in Lent

Because your steadfast love is better than life, my lips will praise you.

Psalm 63:3

Pray
Let my lips praise you, O loving God. May your love be at the center of my life. Amen.

Read
Psalm 63

Reflect
"Thy goodness is better than life" . . . means that it is better than the one thing you still have when you have lost everything, better than your life.

—*Dietrich Bonhoeffer*[26]

Consider
"Better Than Life Itself" (p. 71)

Action Step
List things in your life to release, and think of how God's faithful love sustains you.

Better Than Life Itself

In Lent, we may wonder what we can let go of in life. There are possessions we can give away. There are activities we can let go of and not miss. Perhaps some relationships are ones we could—or should—release. What is left after all of the "leaving go" is finished?

What is left—and what we realize is at the core of life—is the steadfast love of God. God's continuing, nourishing, everlasting love is what we cannot give up because the love of God is better than life itself. The psalmist knew this. Because God's faithful love is better than life, "my lips will praise you."

> **Because God's faithful love is better than life, "my lips will praise you."**

Dietrich Bonhoeffer knew the same thing. He knew that God's goodness is the one thing that is better than all else, and that it will sustain us, even when everything else is gone. When everything is gone, only God's love sustains, for it is the one thing that is better than life itself. Bonhoeffer knew this throughout his life. He surely knew it at the end of life, when he faced a cruel death.

Through Lent we give our praise. We thank God, in gratitude—from the bottom of our hearts—for the steadfast love that never lets us go and never lets us down. We praise and serve our God, whose divine love is better even than our own lives.

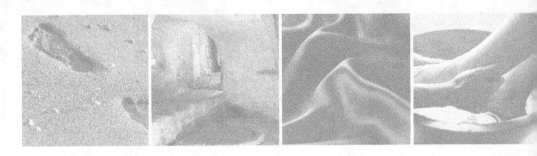

Monday

Praise the Lord! I will give thanks to the Lord with my whole heart.

Psalm 111:1

Pray
We give thanks to you with our whole hearts, O Lord. We praise you! Amen.

Read
Psalm 111

Reflect
Life is for praising the Lord; life arises from praising God.

—Lisa Maugans Driver[27]

Consider
"Praising God" (p. 73)

Action Step
Think about how you can praise God, in various ways; then practice praise in your life.

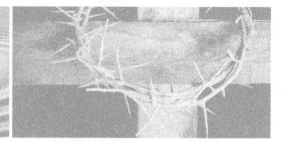

Praising God

When we think about it, much of what we do in life we do in order to gain something else. We work in order to get money in order to spend it as we want. We brush our teeth to avoid tooth decay. We do something for someone so people will think well of us.

But praising God is different. Praising God is something we do for no other reason than that we can praise God. We don't praise to gain anything from God. We don't praise to tell God what we want. We don't have an "agenda" that we want to convey. Praise is the one thing we do without regard for our wants or needs or desired gains. We praise God with our whole heart, because God is God!

Lent is a time for praise. The Psalms are full of psalms of praise that acknowledge God's greatness and goodness and express praise for all God has done for the people of God. This is our highest response to who God is and to what God has done: "Praise the Lord!"

Lisa Maugans Driver tells us that "life is for praising." We are given the gift of life. We receive that gift—and all the gifts we experience in life—from God. God is the source, or fountain, of all goodness for us. So our lives should be spent in praise. We praise God for being God. This is the true life that "arises from praising God." A life without praise is no life at all.

> **God is the source, or fountain, of all goodness for us. So our lives should be spent in praise.**

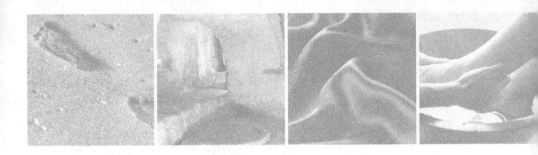

Tuesday

To set the mind on the flesh is death, but to set the mind on the Spirit is life and peace.

Romans 8:6

Pray
O Spirit of God, bring us into the lives you desire for us; make us new. Give us your gift of peace. Amen.

Read
Romans 8:1–11

Reflect
Lent then is a time of affirming that our life according to the flesh is dead, and that new life and peace are available even now through the Spirit of Christ.

—Amy Plantinga Pauw[28]

Consider
"Affirming New Life and Peace" (p. 75)

Action Step
Find ways to express your life in Christ and the peace Christ brings.

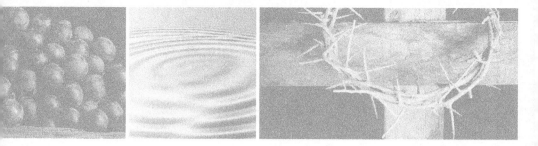

Affirming New Life and Peace

Our Lenten journey is a constant process of looking to what we are "becoming" in Jesus Christ. As Christ's disciples, we always seek his will. For our own lives, we want to know what person Christ wants us to be. This involves listening to God's Spirit, seeking Christ's ways, and looking to the larger purposes of God for us.

We are part of this process of "becoming" because we have turned away from living life on our own. We have said, "No" to ourselves and to our desires for how to live and what to seek. We have said, "Yes" to Christ's call to follow him. This is the contrast of what the New Testament refers to as "flesh" and "spirit." *Flesh* means what we want; *spirit* is what God wants for us.

Amy Plantinga Pauw puts this clearly for us when she notes that Lent means affirming that our life "according to the flesh is dead." We do not give in to our selfish urges. Lent is a time to affirm that "new life and peace" can be and is ours through the Spirit of Christ. The possibilities of becoming who Christ wants us to be, to live in fullness, or "eternal" life, to be at peace with God and with others—all this and more are possible through the Spirit of Christ. Let's live into Lent with new life and peace!

> **Lent means affirming that our life "according to the flesh is dead."**

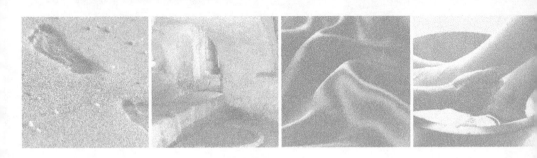

Wednesday

"Repent, and be baptized every one of you in the name of Jesus Christ so that your sins may be forgiven; and you will receive the gift of the Holy Spirit."

Acts 2:38

Pray
We proclaim you, O Christ. Show us ways to say and do what you came to do for us. Amen.

Read
Acts 2:37–42

Reflect
The task of Christians is to proclaim this good news by word of mouth, and to substantiate in their lives the glorious truth that Christ is Victor: that death has been vanquished; that abundant life is to be had; that sins can be forgiven.

—Alan P. F. Sell[29]

Consider
"Living Good News" (p. 77)

Action Step
Today tell someone about Jesus Christ—who he is and what he can do in our lives.

Living Good News

The first converts to Christianity heard Peter's sermon on the Day of Pentecost. He outlined the basics of Christian belief and practice: repentance, baptism in the name of Christ, forgiveness of sins, and the gift of the Holy Spirit. These are still basics for us today.

While our baptism is a one-time occurrence, repentance is continual in our Lenten journey. We look to Jesus Christ, to live in his way. We experience forgiveness when we fall short or turn away from Christ's will for us. We rejoice in God's Spirit given to us for every step along our way.

Alan P. F. Sell captures what this means for us. We Christians proclaim the good news of Christ by what we say. We also live the good news of Jesus Christ in our lives—in what we value and do. We live as though Christ is victor over death—because he is the One who has vanquished our "last enemy." The message of Christ—repentance, forgiveness, baptism, the gift of the Spirit—dwells within us and is the core of who we are and how we live. We are forgiven; we proclaim Christ; we live in the Spirit. This is our faith for all seasons!

> **We live as though Christ is victor over death-because he is the One who has vanquished our "last enemy."**

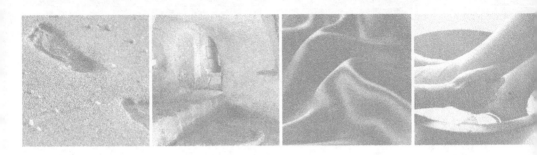

Thursday

And when he had given thanks, he broke it and said, "This is my body that is for you. Do this in remembrance of me."

1 Corinthians 11:24

Pray
Gracious God, you reach out to us in your grace, blessing us. May we express our gratitude from the fullness of our hearts. Amen.

Read
1 Corinthians 11:23–26

Reflect
Grace and gratitude belong together like heaven and earth. Grace evokes gratitude like the voice of an echo. Gratitude follows grace like thunder, lightning. . . . The two belong together, so that only gratitude can correspond to grace, and this correspondence cannot fail.

—Karl Barth[30]

Consider
"Grace and Gratitude" (p. 79)

Action Step
Think of things for which you are grateful. Reflect on the grace of God that provides your source of gratitude.

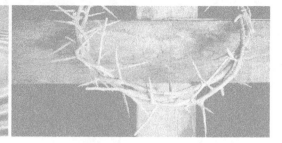

Grace and Gratitude

In some traditions, the Lord's Supper is called the Eucharist. The word *Eucharist* comes from the Greek word *eucharista*, which means "gratitude," "thanksgiving." The Supper is supremely a meal of thanksgiving in which we continually remember the death of Jesus Christ to bring salvation, and in which we continue to receive the benefits of Christ's death for us. Surely, this is the rhythm of our Christian life: grace and gratitude. We receive grace in Jesus Christ, and we express our thanksgiving to God as ever-growing gratitude.

Karl Barth captured this for us in saying that grace and gratitude belong together like heaven and earth. When God speaks—and acts—grace is given, and gratitude is evoked: just like an echo across a deep canyon when one cries out. Gratitude is as sure a response to God's grace as thunder is when lightning occurs.

> **Grace and gratitude belong together like heaven and earth.**

No other response in our lives is adequate for what God has done for us, in the whole history of salvation and most fully in becoming a human in Jesus Christ. Jesus' life, death, and resurrection are the gracious, life-giving actions of the One who loved us and gave himself for us. Our gratitude comes fully and deeply. We express our gratitude most when we commit ourselves to Christ and live as his disciples. Like breathing: we inhale grace and exhale gratitude. This is our life!

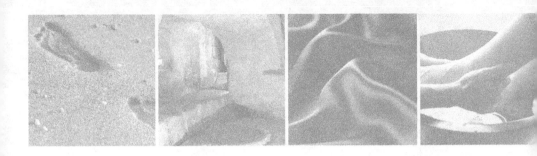

Friday

Those who love me, I will deliver; I will protect those who know my name.

Psalm 91:14

Pray
We entrust ourselves to your care, O Jesus. Be with us, hold us, and keep us in your care. Amen.

Read
Psalm 91

Reflect
When everything you have counted on for protection has failed, the Divine Presence does not fail. The hands are still there—not promising to rescue, not promising to intervene—promising only to hold you no matter how far you fall.

—Barbara Brown Taylor[31]

Consider
"The Divine Presence Holds Us" (p. 81)

Action Step
Think of times in which you have fallen. Reflect on the ways in which God has upheld you and picked you up in Jesus Christ.

The Divine Presence Holds Us

Psalm 91 is one of the great Psalms. It's a deep and meaningful expression of our assurance of God's protection. The people of Israel, in the Old Testament, knew that assurance firsthand. Through all their troubles and dangers, God was there. God protected the nation and those who called out to God for personal help. Surely the Psalmist had that experience. Personal vulnerability and jeopardy may well have been marks of his life.

But the beautiful words of the Psalm were his experience as well. Danger is met by protection. Deliverance from God comes to those who love God; protection to those "who know my name."

Barbara Brown Taylor movingly expresses this trust and assurance. The Divine Presence does not fail. God's hands promise rescue. We are not and cannot be exempt from danger and difficulties. God's "intervention" is not what we experience as much as simply the divine presence. God is there. God holds us. God upholds us no matter the depths to which we descend.

> **God upholds us no matter the depths to which we descend.**

In Lent we know especially God's presence in Jesus Christ. He is "God with us"—Immanuel. Jesus is with us. Jesus is for us. Jesus picks us up, no matter how deep our fall. Jesus is the divine presence who is with us. Jesus assures us we are never alone, never left to ourselves, never in danger that cannot be helped. We trust in him.

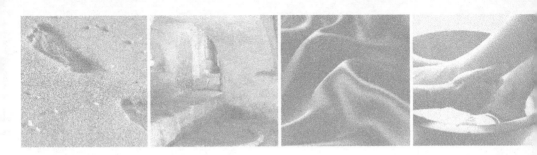

Saturday

So, whether you eat or drink, or whatever you do, do everything for the glory of God.

1 Corinthians 10:31

Pray
May we live for your glory, O God, in all we think, say, and do. Amen.

Read
1 Corinthians 10:31–33

Reflect
And therefore in all our actions we must propound God's glory as the supreme end of them, according to that of the Apostle [1 Cor. 10:31].

—*John Downame*[32]

Consider
"Living for God's Glory" (p. 83)

Action Step
Consider your affections and actions. See if you understand them all as being for the glory of God.

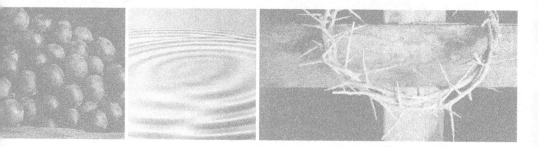

Living for God's Glory

The famous first question of the Westminster Shorter Catechism (1647) asks: What is humanity's chief end? The answer is "to glorify God and to enjoy him forever." A little boy once got the answer wrong and said humanity's chief end was "to glorify God and endure him forever." Some difference!

At least the little boy got the "to glorify God" right. Paul gives us an umbrella, a comprehensive prescription for the Christ life: Whatever we do, do it all for the glory of God.

John Downame said it in the seventeenth century. All of our actions must "propound God's glory" as the supreme "end" or "purpose" of them. This is far-reaching and all-inclusive. No areas of life are exempt from this directive. We cannot hold anything "off limits" from God; we cannot keep some actions "to ourselves." All of life belongs to God; and all of our activities, no matter what, are to be done for God's glory. Do it all for the glory of God.

> **All of life belongs to God; and all of our activities, no matter what, are to be done for God's glory.**

We glorify God when we seek God's direction for our lives and activities. But as we live, we focus what we do—as well as who we are—toward God. We live not for ourselves, but for God. We praise God, worship God, serve God. We are "God-intoxicated," to put it boldly. God pervades us and all we do. We seek not our own praise but the praise of God. We live for God's glory.

Thanking

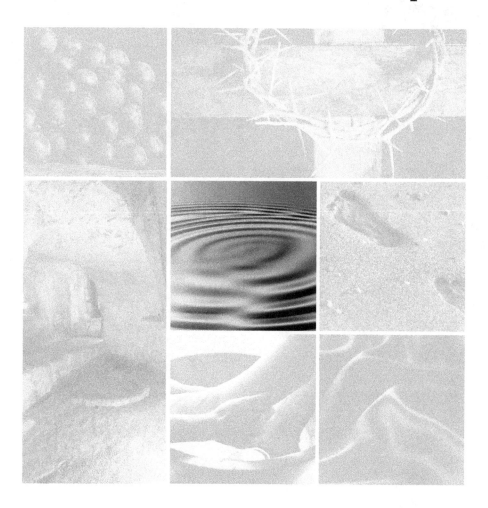

Chapter 6

Enacting
(Fifth Week in Lent)

Enacting

While Lent calls us to "interior practices," such as meditating and prayer, it also beckons us to "outward practices." We live and act in ways that express our Christian discipleship. The inner life and the outward life go together.

On one level, there is "therapy in doing." Those who look within themselves can be depressed or discouraged. So much may seem to be difficult. But those who act may find that the difficulties of the interior life can be helped by involvement in action. When we give ourselves to the needs of others and to purposes beyond ourselves, then things can begin to look different. New perspectives on who we are can open up and lead us to new directions that can invigorate life.

Our Christian faith during Lent can give us even more. In Lent as we express our discipleship in actions, we can find a deeper walk with God as we walk and speak and do for the sake of Jesus Christ and on behalf of others. The "activism" of the Bible shines through when we see people of faith—in Israel and in the church—express the genuineness of their believing by the things they do in the world, for God and for other people. Faith expresses itself in works, to put it theologically. Our acting is inherent in our discipleship. Jesus led his early disciples into preaching, teaching, healing, and serving. He did not withdraw with his band of followers into a permanent retreat. He led them into ministries that brought glory to God and help to those in need in the here and now.

Lent is our time to find these active dimensions of faith. God's Spirit can lead us, open opportunities, and give us the wisdom and courage to venture into new venues of loving God and loving our neighbors.

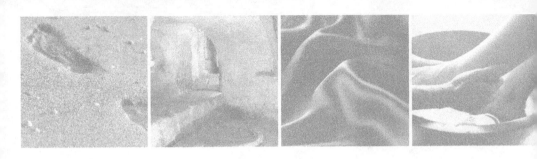

Fifth Sunday in Lent

*Mary took a pound of costly perfume made of pure nard,
anointed Jesus' feet, and wiped them with her hair.*

John 12:3

Pray
Stir me by your Spirit, O Christ, to love and serve you, now. Amen.

Read
John 12:1–8

Reflect
*Mary's declaration for Jesus is not deferred until after his death but is
offered to Jesus while he lives.*

—Gail R. O'Day[33]

Consider
"Do It Now" (p. 89)

Action Step
Think of things you intend to do for Christ and the church, and do
them, now.

Do It Now

As Jesus moved toward the cross, he enjoyed time with his friends, Mary, Martha, and Lazarus. At a dinner for him, Mary performed an extravagant act. She took expensive perfume and anointed Jesus' feet, wiping them with her hair. The fragrance filled the whole house so all could share in this act of love.

Mary was sensitive to Jesus' needs as he came closer to his death. This action, done from the depths of love, was an expression of profound care, lovingly performed at a time when Jesus' human needs were strong, and when he was in the midst of those friends whom he loved so deeply.

Gail O'Day points out that Mary did not wait until after Jesus was dead to declare love for Jesus or to provide an expression of love. Mary conveyed extravagant love while Jesus was still alive, when it met his need, when it meant the most. She did it now, not deferring until later.

Contrast Mary's anointing with a pound of perfume with the hundred pounds of myrrh and aloes that Nicodemus brought to anoint Jesus' body after his death (John 19:39). The gifts are disproportionate in size. But Mary's one pound was given when Jesus could receive it.

> **Mary conveyed extravagant love while Jesus was still alive, when it met his need, when it meant the most.**

In Lent, we should "do it now." We should anoint, love, and serve Jesus, before it is too late.

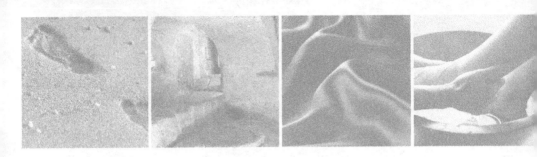

Monday

You see that faith was active along with his works, and faith was brought to completion by the works.

James 2:22

Pray
Increase our faith, O Christ, and increase what we do, as being done for you. Amen.

Read
James 2:14–26

Reflect
We do not become righteous by doing righteous deeds but, having been made righteous, we do righteous deeds.

—Martin Luther[34]

Consider
"Doing Righteous Deeds" (p. 91)

Action Step
List ways in which you put your faith into action by what you do.

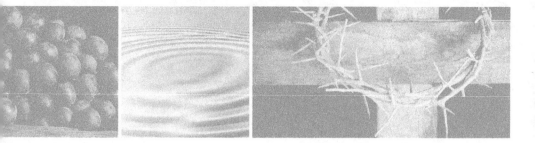

Doing Righteous Deeds

Martin Luther's opinion of the Letter of James is well-known. He called it an "epistle of straw" because he read the book as teaching salvation by works. For Luther, the emphasis on deeds overshadowed what he believed was the primary New Testament teaching from the apostle Paul: We are saved by faith, not by works.

But reading James aright shows that he recognizes Paul's notion of faith and expands it. We are saved from sin and its power by faith in Jesus Christ. But this faith is not purely an intellectual belief. It is an active engagement of the whole self. We *believe* in Jesus Christ; then we live out our faith in what we do. If our faith is not this kind of active faith, it is not true faith at all.

> **We *believe* in Jesus Christ; then we live out our faith in what we do.**

Luther captured this in writing against defective theology. He issued the warning that we do not become righteous by doing righteous deeds. We can't ingratiate ourselves to God by trying to do good works. But having been made righteous through Jesus Christ, as Luther would put it, we do righteous deeds. Our works are the outcome, or result, of our faith. So our faith, to be complete, must be alive and active in the world, expressing itself not just in what we say, but also in what we do. We show the genuineness of our believing by our living.

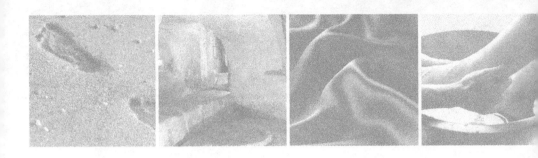

Tuesday

*Let the wicked forsake their way, and the unrighteous their
thoughts; let them return to the Lord, that he may have mercy
on them, and to our God, for he will abundantly pardon.*

Isaiah 55:7

Pray
*Turn us around, O God. Lead us to repent . . . and repent . . . and
repent. Amen.*

Read
Isaiah 55:6–9

Reflect
*Accordingly, we must strive toward repentance itself, devote ourselves
to it throughout life, and pursue it to the very end if we would abide
in Christ.*

—John Calvin[35]

Consider
"Repenting Throughout Life" (p. 93)

Action Step
Reflect on your understanding of repentance. Consider the ways in
which you continually repent and the differences that this repenting
makes for you.

Repenting Throughout Life

The word *repent* is important during Lent. In Hebrew, it literally means "to turn around." In Greek, it means "to change one's mind." In Latin, "to do penance." Therefore, we can see the different dimensions of meaning that surround the word as we use it today.

Repenting means change. It is turning around and walking in a new direction in life. If we are following paths of sin, we turn toward the paths of righteousness. If we are walking in the ways of self-aggrandizement and self-exaltation, we turn toward the ways of God and of serving other people. As an old jingle puts it: "It's not enough to say, / 'I'm sorry and repent,' / And then to go on afterwards / Just as you always went." Repenting means new directions.

John Calvin saw this when he recognized that repentance must be an ongoing process. It goes on throughout our whole lives as we constantly try to know God's way and follow it, rather than pursue our own paths. Repentance is an early act of the Christian life and continues as an ongoing process, pursued to the very end of life. Repentance is not a "set it and forget it" form of Christian devotion. It is action. We repent repeatedly as we turn around and find God's way set before us.

> **Repentance is an early act of the Christian life and continues as an ongoing process, pursued to the very end of life.**

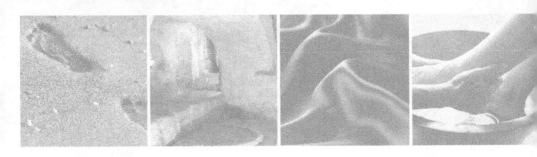

Wednesday

The earth is the LORD's and all that is in it, the world, and those who live in it.

Psalm 24:1

Pray
We praise you for the greatness and goodness of the earth, O Creator God. May we be wise and faithful stewards of all we have been given. Amen.

Read
Psalm 24

Reflect
We are challenged to be faithful, wise, trustworthy, and hardworking stewards of the wonderfully fruitful earth that God has entrusted to our care.

—Henry G. Brinton[36]

Consider
"Caring for the Earth" (p. 95)

Action Step
Find practical ways to care for the earth. As a place to start, consider changing your practices regarding energy usage.

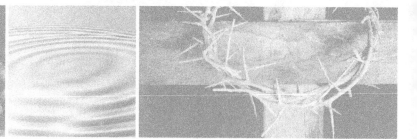

Caring for the Earth

It is hard to imagine a more comprehensive claim than this verse from the psalmist. God is the Lord of the earth. God is the Lord of all that is in the earth. What more can be said?

Since the earth and all that is in it is created by God and belongs to God, our human participation on the earth comes with certain recognitions. One is that we, too, belong to God. We are dependent on God; we trust God.

However, a second recognition is that the earth we have been given, as a gift from God, is to be treated by humans in ways that acknowledge that ultimately the earth is the Lord's. We are not free to treat the earth however we please. This is the responsibility of stewardship.

Henry G. Brinton describes the kinds of stewards we should be concerning the earth. We should be faithful—in seeking and carrying out God's will for the earth and for how the earth is used. We should be wise—in planning for the earth's welfare. We should be trustworthy—in using our gifts from God in the best possible ways for God's glory. We should be hardworking—in continuing to be dedicated to doing what needs to be done to insure the continuation of the wonderfully fruitful earth God has given us. While humans may be "over nature," we are always "under God."

> **While humans may be "over nature," we are always "under God."**

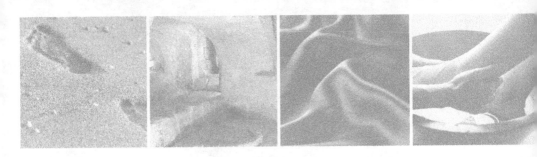

Thursday

Happy are those whose help is the God of Jacob, . . . who executes justice for the oppressed; who gives food to the hungry.

Psalm 146:5–7

Pray
O just God, teach us what your justice is and how it can be shared in situations where there is great need. Amen.

Read
Psalm 146

Reflect
When we perform deeds of justice, we are alive; when we sin, we cease to be.

—Jerome[37]

Consider
"Doing Justice" (p. 97)

Action Step
Reflect on the relationship between God's justice and our human attempts at justice. Find places or situations where you can work on behalf of God's justice.

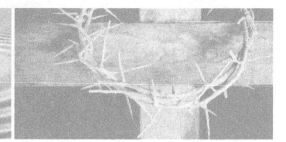

Doing Justice

Establishing justice for those who are deprived of justice is what God does. We may not think of this too often. But all through the Old Testament, it is clear that God seeks justice for those who are oppressed (see Deuteronomy 10:18; Psalm 82:3; Isaiah 1:17). This justice is an expression of God's mercy and righteousness.

This is plain from Psalm 146. True happiness belongs to those "whose help is the God of Jacob, whose hope is in the LORD their God" (v. 5). This God is the maker of heaven and earth, who "keeps faith forever" (v. 6). The great Creator God is the one who can give help. This God is forever faithful and can be trusted to give help. This God carries out justice for those who are oppressed and feeds the hungry. Doing justice is a priority for God since this is God's character.

> **Doing justice is a priority for God since this is God's character.**

Our human character is like God's when we do justice too. Jerome, in the early Christian centuries, said that doing deeds of justice makes us "alive." This is because we are living in the ways God wants, in the ways God lives. When we turn away from this commitment to justice, we sin and so we "cease to be." This puts justice high in our priorities. We seek the alleviation of others' needs since they are our concerns, and they are our concerns because they are God's concerns.

Friday

"The second is this, 'You shall love your neighbor as yourself.'"

Mark 12:31

Pray

We say we love you, O God. Help us to express our love for you by loving our neighbors—no matter who they are. Amen.

Read

Mark 12:28–34

Reflect

As the one who loves God you cannot do otherwise. As you love God, you will love your neighbor; the one who with you is loved by God and loves Him in return.

—Karl Barth[38]

Consider

"Loving Neighbors" (p. 99)

Action Step

Consider people in society about whom you seldom think, as your neighbors. See if there are hands-on ways you can express love for them.

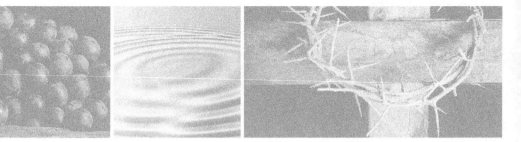

Loving Neighbors

Jesus summarized the Old Testament law rather neatly: Love God and love your neighbor. If everybody lived this way, the world would certainly be different!

These two dimensions of life go together. We love God, our creator and redeemer. God's love is known in Jesus Christ. As we love him and follow him, we are loving the God who first loved us (1 John 4:19).

We love our neighbor who, according to Jesus' most famous parable, the Good Samaritan, is anyone in need (Luke 10:25–37). You can't have one kind of love without the other. Our love extends in all directions: "upward" to God and "outward" to our neighbors.

Karl Barth reminded us of the expression of love of neighbor that is inevitably linked to our love of God. If we love God, we cannot do anything else than love our neighbor. Remember that the neighbor is like us. God loves us both. Therefore, we are bound to others with the strongest relationship. Our creator mutually loves us.

> **If we love God, we cannot do anything else than love our neighbor.**

We are also united with neighbors who share a love for God in return. Our love for God liberates us to love others also, to be "for others." Mutual love between neighbors and us is made possible by our mutual love of God. We serve our neighbors, we care for our neighbors and love our neighbors because we are united by the deepest reality we know in life: the love of God in Jesus Christ.

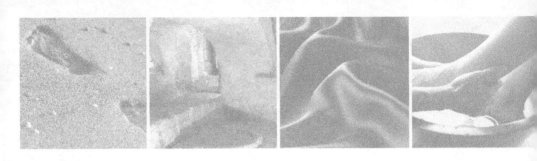

Saturday

All this is from God, who reconciled us to himself through Christ, and has given us the ministry of reconciliation.

2 Corinthians 5:18

Pray
O God, you have reconciled us in Jesus Christ. Reenergize us as a community of reconciliation in a world where needs are great. Amen.

Read
2 Corinthians 5:16–21

Reflect
To be reconciled to God is to be sent into the world as God's reconciling community.

—The Confession of 1967[39]

Consider
"Reconciling" (p. 101)

Action Step
Think of your church's activities in mission and ministry. List them and describe how they help reconciliation take place.

Reconciling

Certainly, this passage from 2 Corinthians is one of the key New Testament passages that proclaim the work of Jesus Christ. Reconciliation. This one word is central to the gospel message. It captures the glorious message that in Jesus Christ, reconciliation has taken place between the world and God, and between people themselves. It is hard to imagine a greater word of "good news" than this!

We sometimes emphasize the reconciliation with God that we have in Christ while neglecting where this leads us. Our reconciliation with God leads us to the work of reconciliation with others. Surely, this is deeply needed at every turn. The news of any day in the world or in our communities shows how crucial the needs for reconciliation are.

> **The news of any day in the world or in our communities shows how crucial the needs for reconciliation are.**

During Lent in our churches, we can recognize that this is one of the main identifying marks of the Christian community. The Confession of 1967 prompts us to realize that our reconciliation with God propels us as the church into the world to be a reconciling community. As the body of Christ, we are to embody the reconciliation God has given in Christ, to others. The church community itself is composed of those reconciled to God. We are to demonstrate that reconciliation and to engage in reconciling activities at every level, in every situation.

To be reconcilers is a mark of Christian discipleship. To be a community of reconciliation is to be sent on God's mission in this world. It is to minister in the name of Christ, who has made us one in him.

Chapter 7

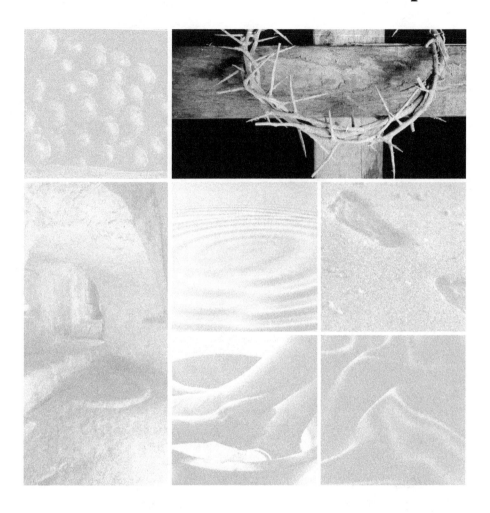

Gathering at the Cross
(Holy Week)

Gathering at the Cross

The cross of Jesus Christ is the central symbol of Christianity. It stands at the center of our faith, the image that brings to us the fullness of salvation that Jesus attained for us through his death (Romans 5:8). The cross is the sign of God's love, a love so deep that we can never comprehend its depth or full significance (John 3:16). When we look at the cross, we can say, "God loves like that!"

The ministry of Jesus proceeded through his deeds of love and mercy. At one point in the Gospel of Luke, we read: "When the days drew near for him to be taken up, he set his face to go to Jerusalem" (Luke 9:51). We can see this verse as a key, a pivotal point in this Gospel. It is clear that Jesus is on his way to danger, on his way to his death on the cross. He chose this path, willingly. He followed this path, obediently. Though he was innocent, he was crucified as guilty in the eyes of his enemies. But his crucifixion led to his resurrection. It led to reconciliation and new life for the world. Out of the worst injustice and tragedy imaginable, the most meaningful and life-changing reality came to be. Now salvation has come; liberation from sin and death brings us eternal life.

As we contemplate dimensions of the cross, we find the wondrous drama of God's grace and love. The cross where the Son of God died for us brings us to the heart of our faith, for here the heart of God is given to us and for us. Here we see how much God loved the world and how much God loves us.

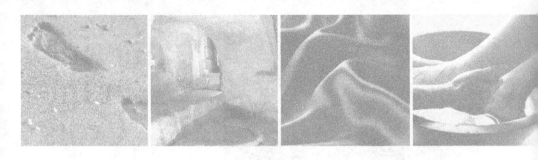

Passion/Palm Sunday

Then Jesus, crying with a loud voice, said, "Father, into your hands I commend my spirit." Having said this, he breathed his last.

Luke 23:46

Pray
Lord Jesus Christ, thank you for giving your life for the world. Thank you for giving your life for me. Amen.

Read
Luke 23:1–49

Reflect
What is sacrificial about Jesus' life and death is that Jesus pours out the superabundance of his life into our life, overcoming our death with life, lack with abundance, debt with grace.

—Sally A. Brown[40]

Consider
"His Life Poured Out" (p. 107)

Action Step
Think of the ways your life is made new by the love you experience in Jesus Christ.

His Life Poured Out

Holy Week begins with the Sunday called both Passion Sunday and Palm Sunday. Crowds who hailed Jesus on Palm Sunday saw him nailed to the cross at the end of the week. The hymn "Ride On! Ride On in Majesty!" captures these two dimensions: "In lowly pomp ride on to die." Jesus' life in these days moved toward the full expression of his passion, his suffering and death on the cross.

On the cross, Jesus breathed his last. His cry was to God, into whose hands he entrusted his life. Then death came. Yet from this death came new life for those who see in the death of Jesus Christ God's inexhaustible love reaching out to reconcile and restore us to the relationship of love and trust God intends to have with us as God's people.

Sally A. Brown interprets the sacrificial nature of Jesus' death by seeing it as his self-donation, his self-giving. He poured his life into our lives, filling our lives with newness we could never imagine. Jesus gave himself up to death, for us. His death overcomes our death so we have new life. All our lacks are made up for by the abundance Jesus gives. All our debts to God are met by the grace of Christ's love so we can now live in freedom and forgiveness.

All our debts to God are met by the grace of Christ's love so we can now live in freedom and forgiveness.

We enter Holy Week in awe and wonder at God's amazing love, poured out for us in Jesus Christ.

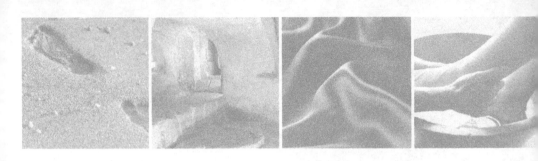

Holy Monday

*He has rescued us from the power of darkness and transferred us
into the kingdom of his beloved Son, in whom we have redemption,
the forgiveness of sins.*

Colossians 1:13–14

Pray
*O Jesus Christ, you have joined yourself with us in becoming one of
us. You have cared for us so much that you have died for us. Accept
our deepest thankfulness. Amen.*

Read
Colossians 1:9–14

Reflect
*As we see in the incarnation itself, God is not removed from suffering,
but God's care for us—and for the world—is seen in the cross.*

—Catherine Gunsalus González[41]

Consider
"God's Care in the Cross" (p. 109)

Action Step
Reflect on what the cross of Jesus Christ means to you, especially
as an expression of God's care.

God's Care in the Cross

Christmas is the celebration of God becoming a human in Jesus Christ, the incarnation. Good Friday recognizes the love and care for the world that God has in Jesus Christ, who died that our sin may be forgiven.

Given who we are, as sinners who have lived in our own ways, broken God's laws, and failed to be who God wants us to be, we need redemption. We need our sin to be forgiven and our lives made new and liberated from the power of sin. This is what Jesus has done for us on the cross. Through his death, we are set free from the control of sin over us and given the freedom that only forgiveness of sin can bring.

> **Through his death, we are set free from the control of sin over us and given the freedom that only forgiveness of sin can bring.**

Catherine Gunsalus González reminds us that forgiveness and liberation come to us in the cross. Here we see God's care for us. It was love that led Jesus to die for us. Jesus' suffering love can set us free. In becoming a human, Jesus gave himself into the fullness of our humanity, of who we are. This embeds him, in his incarnation, in the suffering we face in this world. Now, in the cross, that same care and love are given. Through Jesus' death, we are forgiven. Our lives can be redeemed, made new. Our world has a future that is transformed by God's everlasting love in Jesus Christ (John 3:16). In this Holy Week, we look to God's care in the cross.

Holy Tuesday

But God proves his love for us in that while we still were sinners Christ died for us.

Romans 5:8

Pray

Eternal God, you love us with an eternal love. In your Son, may we experience your love wrapped around us and holding us to you. Amen.

Read

Romans 5:6–11

Reflect

In discoursing of the love that was shown in the Cross of Christ the New Testament is never able to stop short of tracing it up-stream to the eternal love of God dealing sacrificially with the sins of the world.

—Donald M. Baillie[42]

Consider

"The Eternal Love of God" (p. 111)

Action Step

Think about all the relationships of love in your life and give thanks for each one. Think about the eternal love of God, expressed in Jesus Christ. And thank God.

The Eternal Love of God

Jesus' crucifixion appeared the same as all the hundreds of other crucifixions carried out by Roman soldiers. The same procedure was used; the same tortures inflicted. Jesus of Nazareth experienced the same pains as all other Roman victims.

Yet for us, the death of Jesus was also like no other death. The death of Jesus is the unique expression of God's love for us as sinful humans. His death was "for us," on our behalf, for our benefit. His death saves us from sin and its power. His death was just what we needed. He was given for us when we needed it most—"while we still were sinners."

Donald Baillie points to the fact that the New Testament describes the love shown to us in the cross of Christ as originating in God's eternal love. In the cross, God proves or shows this eternal love in the sacrifice of the Son of God, Jesus Christ, as the way by which our sin is forgiven. No other sacrifice could have done what Jesus did. No other person could have demonstrated God's love in the same way.

> **The New Testament describes the love shown to us in the cross of Christ as originating in God's eternal love.**

God loves us eternally in Jesus Christ. Now and forever, we are held in this love and are forgiven in this love.

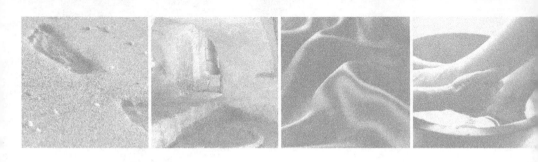

Holy Wednesday

And when you were dead in trespasses and the uncircumcision of your flesh, God made you alive together with him, when he forgave us all our trespasses.

Colossians 2:13

Pray
You meet us at the point of our greatest need, O loving God. Forgive us in Christ, for all our sin. Amen.

Read
Colossians 2:8–15

Reflect
Jesus taught God's gracious forgiveness and practiced that forgiveness throughout his ministry. The cross of Jesus highlights God's forgiving heart toward sinners or oppressors.

—Andrew Sung Park[43]

Consider
"God's Forgiving Heart" (p. 113)

Action Step
In the midst of Holy Week, think of the forgiveness we receive through the death of Christ on the cross. Resolve to forgive others today, and ask for forgiveness from others.

God's Forgiving Heart

In the cross of Jesus Christ, God did something for us that we could not do for ourselves. The Scriptures indicate we sinners are "dead in trespasses" (cf. Ephesians 2:1). We are completely cut off from God, unable to help ourselves. We can never reach out to establish a relationship with God by our own powers. Dead means dead!

But God has acted. God has taken the initiative to change our human situation. Through the cross, God has made us alive with Christ. The dead have come alive! Now we can share in Christ's life. We can share in Christ's life because through the cross, God forgives us of all—imagine that, *all!*—our trespasses. Now we can receive the relationship of faith and trust, love and fellowship that God has desired from humans from the very start. The cross makes all the difference. We have new life in Jesus Christ.

Andrew Sung Park points out that Jesus practiced forgiveness throughout his ministry. Jesus spoke forgiveness and lived forgiveness. The cross is where we see forgiveness in action. God's forgiving heart reaches out through the cross to embrace us. God's forgiving heart receives both sinners and oppressors. We who sin and we who oppress are forgiven and are made alive in and with Christ. Only God in Christ could have done this for us. Only in Christ is forgiveness to be found and new life become possible.

God's forgiving heart reaches out through the cross to embrace us.

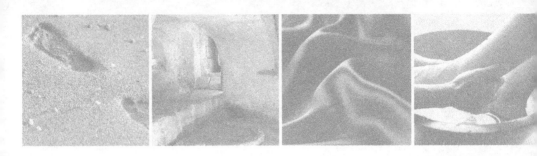

Maundy Thursday

For the wages of sin is death, but the free gift of God is eternal life in Christ Jesus our Lord.

Romans 6:23

Pray
May we live in the light of your forgiveness, O Christ. Free us from guilt. Give us lives of freedom, expressed in love for you and for others. Amen.

Read
Romans 6:15–23

Reflect
By forgiving us, he relieves us, not of the consequences of our sins but of the consequences of being sinners.

—William Sloane Coffin[44]

Consider
"Christ's Forgiveness" (p. 115)

Action Step
Think of the sin and misdeeds of your life. Pray to God for forgiveness. Find ways to live as a free person in Christ, with sin forgiven.

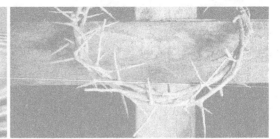

Christ's Forgiveness

The seriousness with which the Bible takes sin is captured in the image of "death." Paul indicates that the outcome of our condition as sinners is that we lose our lives. We lose our relationship of life with God—which is what true life is. We are cut off from God so radically that "death" is the only term that is strong enough to describe our situation.

But God brings us to life! God gives us a gift, which is new life—eternal life—in Jesus Christ, our Lord. This is pure grace. We now have a new status and a new relationship with God. We are "alive to God in Christ Jesus" (Romans 6:11). We have eternal life, instead of **God brings us to life!** eternal death. We receive not what we deserve, but what God gives. Now life can be lived in the freedom of forgiveness and fellowship with God through Jesus Christ.

William Sloane Coffin points out that by forgiving us, God in Christ does not take away the results of our sins. These may endure. But what we receive is freedom from the results of being sinners. We are now forgiven sinners. We live in a relationship of faith and trust in Jesus Christ, united with him, and are those who have received eternal life, right here, right now. This is the greatest new life imaginable!

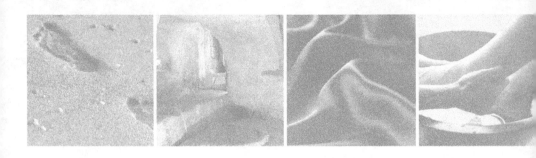

Good Friday

And through him God was pleased to reconcile to himself
all things, whether on earth or in heaven, by making peace
through the blood of his cross.

Colossians 1:20

Pray
Bring us together in your love, O Christ. May hurts be healed and
wholeness be found. Amen.

Read
Colossians 1:15–20

Reflect
All the dualisms which divide, separate, cause pain, and support
oppression and lack of communion with the other are all gathered
together at the crucifixion, and Christ receives them. . . . Everything
converges in him, and in his power and activity everything finds
wholeness and meaning.

—Patricia Wilson-Kastner[45]

Consider
"All Separation Overcome in Christ" (p. 117)

Action Step
Think of separations that are part of your life. Based on the cross of
Christ, take steps today to overcome divisions and to be reconciled.

All Separation Overcome in Christ

The power of Jesus' crucifixion goes beyond us, ourselves. It reaches out to affect the whole creation. The majestic statement in Colossians is that through Christ God reconciles "all things" to God and makes peace. The phrase *all things* encompasses not just the created order on earth but also the heavens. We can only envision what all these things are. But the crucifixion has cosmic significance. It brings peace. The crucifixion has ramifications we can only imagine.

Patricia Wilson-Kastner helps us see that, in the crucifixion, the dualisms that divide us are overcome. We have "either/or" situations all around us, usually in tension or hostility, bringing pain and dividing people. Race, gender, politics, religion—all that set people against each other are "gathered together at the crucifixion," and Christ receives them. If Christ takes them on himself, then we no longer have to let them have power over us. We do not have to let them divide. We are reconciled, and so should be our differences when they separate, oppress, and breed anger and disrespect. Everything converges in Christ and in him finds wholeness and meaning. The power of Christ's cross to bring together all that separates is part of Christ's cosmic work. Jesus Christ reconciles!

> **Everything converges in Christ and in him finds wholeness and meaning.**

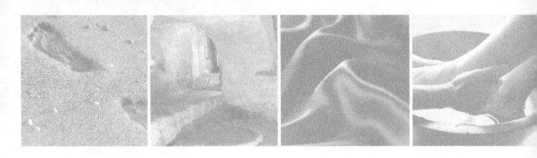

Holy Saturday

Then Jesus said, "Father, forgive them; for they do not know what they are doing."

Luke 23:34

Pray
Thank you, Lord Jesus, for taking my judgment upon yourself and for giving me grace that overflows throughout my life. Amen.

Read
Luke 23:32–38

Reflect
All sound Christian theology begins and ends at the foot of the cross. It is the single event in the Gospels that unveils the full depth and horror of human sin and the radical nature of God's grace and love.

—George W. Stroup[46]

Consider
"Our Sin and God's Grace" (p. 119)

Action Step
Recognize the judgment you rightly deserve. Recognize the grace of God in Jesus Christ that takes judgment and gives wondrous grace.

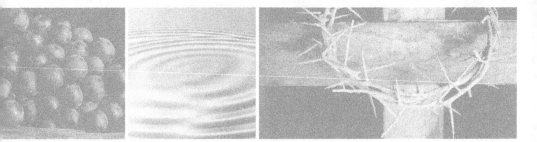

Our Sin and God's Grace

The cross of Jesus Christ reveals both judgment and grace. It is judgment on the world's sin and on the sin that put the innocent Son of God to death. In his death, Jesus absorbed God's judgment on human sin and took it upon himself.

The cross of Jesus Christ also reveals God's grace. God took the initiative in sending Jesus Christ into the world to die for us. In the cross is revealed the overflowing love of God in giving us what we do not deserve—and not giving us what we do deserve. This is grace. It is the grace Jesus utters: "Forgive them, for they do not know what they are doing." The gracious word for us is the word of forgiveness.

George Stroup speaks of the radical nature of the crucifixion. The cross reveals the depth and horror of our sin. Yet it also presents us with the radical nature of the grace and love of God. On the cross, Jesus absorbs human sin and transforms the cross from an instrument of death to a symbol of new life.

> On the cross, Jesus absorbs human sin and transforms the cross from an instrument of death to a symbol of new life.

Our sin and God's grace meet on the cross. They meet when Jesus Christ takes on our judgment. They meet when Jesus Christ, as the grace of God, assures us of God's everlasting love.

Sessions for Group Study

Following Jesus
(Week of Ash Wednesday)

MAIN IDEA

Jesus calls us. He invites us to respond, to be his followers, to commit our lives to him, to live in obedience to his will and his way. Our Lenten journey is a time of focusing strongly on what it means to be a disciple, or follower, of Jesus Christ.

PREPARING TO LEAD

- Read "Following Jesus (Week of Ash Wednesday)" on pages 3–11.
- Read this study session and select questions and activities that you will use. What other questions, issues, or themes occur to you from your reflection?
- Each session includes a hymn. Provide copies of your congregation's hymnal. If you do not have a piano or keyboard and someone to play, consider asking someone to record the music to help the group sing the hymn.

GATHERING

- Provide name tags and pens as people arrive.
- Provide simple refreshments; ask a volunteer to bring refreshments next week.
- Since this is the first session, agree on simple "ground rules" and logistics; e.g., time to begin and end the session; location for

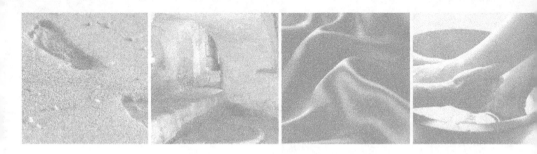

meetings; welcoming of all points of view; confidentiality, etc. Encourage participants to bring their study books and Bibles.

- Review the format for these sessions: Gathering, Opening Worship, Conversation, and Conclusion.

OPENING WORSHIP

Prayer (unison)
O Lord Jesus Christ, be with us and lead us in your way, helping us to trust you as we go. Amen.

Lectio Divina (reflective or prayerful reading)
Read Luke 5:1–11 aloud. Invite all to reflect for a few minutes in silence.

After reflection time, invite all to listen for a word or phrase as the passage is read again and to reflect on that word or phrase in silence.

Read the passage a third time, asking all to offer a silent prayer following the reading.

Invite volunteers to share the word or phrase that spoke most deeply to them.

Prayer
Loving God, hear our prayers today as we seek to follow you more faithfully:
(spoken prayers may be offered)
O Lord Jesus, help us know the opportunity of discipleship so that as we follow you, we will experience the true life you want us to have as your disciples. Hear us now as we pray together, saying, Our Father . . .

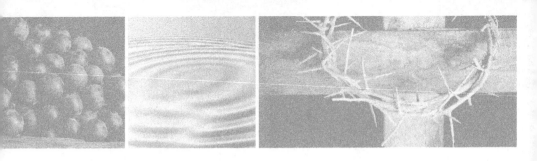

CONVERSATION

- Review the daily readings in "Following Jesus (pages 4–11). Share observations, reflections, and insights on the readings.
- Invite each member of the group briefly to share a "call story," a moment, a relationship, or an event that helped confirm their identities. Then reflect on common themes or characteristics from these stories.
- Note that the story of the call of the disciples is one of the most significant images of God's call to faithful living. Ask: Why is it so memorable? What were some of your reflections on that story? What does it tell us about God?
- Invite members of the group to name ways in which following Jesus brings them joy. Invite them to think of times when Christ's mercy has brought them joy.

CONCLUSION

Prayer
The Lord be with you.
    And also with you.
Help us to know the joy of being your disciples, O Christ. Help us to face the future with the assurance of your mercy. Amen.

Hymn
"Jesus Calls Us"

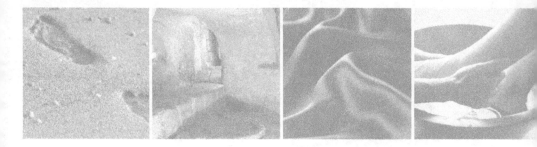

Meditating (First Week in Lent)

MAIN IDEA

Lent gives us opportunities to meditate on the Word of God in Scripture, through which we encounter who God is and the ways God has acted in this world. We meditate on our faith, what we believe. We reflect on our lives and on the ways faith affects our lives in many ways, every day.

PREPARING TO LEAD

- Read "Meditating (First Week in Lent)" on pages 15–29.
- Read this study session and select questions and activities that you will use. What other questions, issues, or themes occur to you from your reflection?
- Each session includes a hymn. Provide copies of your congregation's hymnal. If you do not have a piano or keyboard and someone to play, consider asking someone to record the music to help the group sing the hymn.

GATHERING

- Provide name tags and pens as people arrive.
- Provide simple refreshments if other arrangements for refreshments have not been made; ask a volunteer to bring refreshments next week.

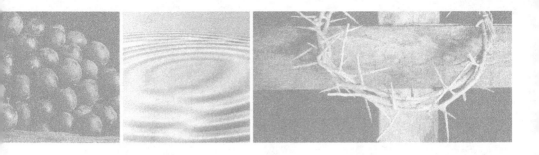

- Review the "ground rules" and logistics; e.g., time to begin and end the session; location for meetings; welcoming of all points of view; confidentiality, etc. Encourage participants to bring their study books and Bibles.
- Review the format for these sessions: Gathering, Opening Worship, Conversation, and Conclusion.

OPENING WORSHIP

Prayer (unison)
O God, help us to know you. In knowing you, may we love you, serve you, and be your faithful people. Amen.

Lectio Divina (reflective or prayerful reading)
Read Psalm 37:1–7 aloud. Invite all to reflect for a few minutes in silence.

After reflection time, invite all to listen for a word or phrase as the passage is read again and to reflect on that word or phrase in silence.

Read the passage a third time, asking all to offer a silent prayer following the reading.

Invite volunteers to share the word or phrase that spoke most deeply to them.

Prayer
Loving God, hear our prayers today as we seek to follow you more faithfully:
(spoken prayers may be offered)
O God, our hearts are restless until they find their rest in you. May our hearts rest in you, by faith. Hear us now as we pray together, saying, Our Father . . .

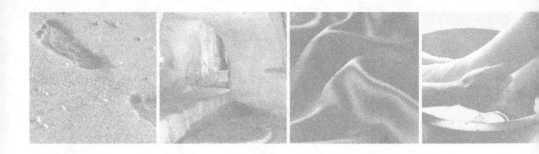

CONVERSATION

- Review the daily readings in "Meditating" (pages 16–29). Share observations, reflections, and insights on the readings.
- Invite each member of the group briefly to describe ways in which faith engages their minds, comforts their hearts, and engages their hands in actions.
- Reflect on the following statement by John Calvin: "This is the main purpose of the Gospel, that, although we are by nature children of wrath, the quarrel between God and us can be resolved and he can receive us into His grace." Invite group members to offer their versions of the main purpose of the gospel. Then reflect on common themes or characteristics of their responses.
- Consider the differences between comfort based on "hoping for the best" compared with the comfort of faith grounded in the actions of God. Invite the group to write a prayer thanking God for their comfort.

CONCLUSION

Prayer

The Lord be with you.
   And also with you.
O triune God—Father, Son, and Holy Spirit—hold us in your hands, protect us, and comfort us, always. Amen.

Hymn

"Come, Ye Faithful, Raise the Strain"

Praying
(Second Week in Lent)

MAIN IDEA

Prayer is conversation with God. It is a true expression of who we are, of what we are thinking and feeling. In prayer, we "let it all hang out" before the One who calls us to prayer and invites us to pray in such a way that prayer becomes as natural to us as breathing.

PREPARING TO LEAD

- Read "Praying (Second Week in Lent)" on pages 33–47.
- Read this study session and select questions and activities that you will use. What other questions, issues, or themes occur to you from your reflection?
- Each session includes a hymn. Provide copies of your congregation's hymnal. If you do not have a piano or keyboard and someone to play, consider asking someone to record the music to help the group sing the hymn.

GATHERING

- Provide name tags and pens as people arrive.
- Provide simple refreshments if other arrangements for refreshments have not been made; ask a volunteer to bring refreshments next week.
- Review the "ground rules" and logistics; e.g., time to begin and

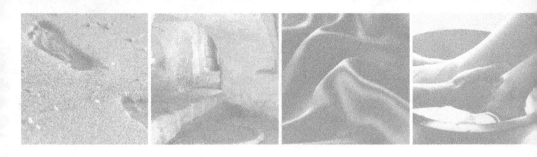

end the session; location for meetings; welcoming of all points of view; confidentiality, etc. Encourage participants to bring their study books and Bibles.

- Review the format for these sessions: Gathering, Opening Worship, Conversation, and Conclusion.

OPENING WORSHIP

Prayer (unison)
Hear our prayers and answer us according to your grace, O God.
Hear our prayers to do your will. Amen.

Lectio Divina (reflective or prayerful reading)
Read Psalm 62 aloud. Invite all to reflect for a few minutes in silence.

After reflection time, invite all to listen for a word or phrase as the passage is read again and to reflect on that word or phrase in silence.

Read the passage a third time, asking all to offer a silent prayer following the reading.

Invite volunteers to share the word or phrase that spoke most deeply to them.

Prayer
Loving God, hear our prayers today as we seek to follow you more faithfully:
(spoken prayers may be offered)
Keep us awake and praying, O Lord—awake to see what you are doing in this world, and praying, always, to know your will and to do it. Hear us now as we pray together, saying, Our Father . . .

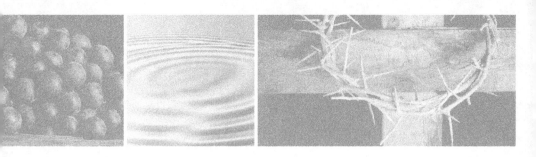

CONVERSATION

- Review the daily readings in "Praying" (pages 34–47). Share observations, reflections, and insights on the readings.
- Invite each member of the group briefly to share something about their prayer lives. Then reflect on common themes or characteristics from these stories.
- Reflect on the following statement by Daniel Migliore: "The practice of Christian prayer, however, cannot be separated from service and work for God's reign. Praying is always to be accompanied by working. Christians do not pray rather than work, or work rather than pray. The practice of Christian hope requires both. Prayer inspires service, and service always begins and ends in prayer." Invite the group members to consider ways in which their own actions can become a part of their prayers.
- Invite members of the group to name ways in which praying is a conversation with God. Invite them to think of times when prayer has brought them a greater sense of who God is.

CONCLUSION

Prayer
The Lord be with you.
And also with you.
Loving God, help us to be loving toward others and to overcome difficult relationships through prayer. Give us eyes to see injustices and give us the will to pray and to work against injustices. Amen.

Hymn
"Prayer Is the Soul's Sincere Desire"

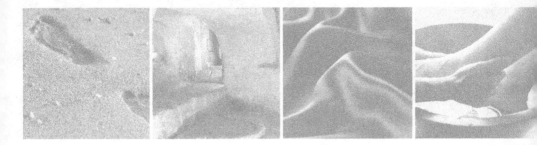

Loving
(Third Week in Lent)

MAIN IDEA

We pursue love, in all ways—love for enemies, for the church, for all in the world—because God has loved us with a deep and everlasting love in Jesus Christ. In the words of the First Letter of John: "Beloved, since God loved us so much, we also ought to love one another" (1 John 4:11).

PREPARING TO LEAD

- Read "Loving (Third Week in Lent)" on pages 51–65.
- Read this study session and select questions and activities that you will use. What other questions, issues, or themes occur to you from your reflection?
- Each session includes a hymn. Provide copies of your congregation's hymnal. If you do not have a piano or keyboard and someone to play, consider asking someone to record the music to help the group sing the hymn.

GATHERING

- Provide name tags and pens as people arrive.
- Provide simple refreshments if other arrangements for refreshments have not been made; ask a volunteer to bring refreshments next week.

- Review the "ground rules" and logistics; e.g., time to begin and end the session; location for meetings; welcoming of all points of view; confidentiality, etc. Encourage participants to bring their study books and Bibles.
- Review the format for these sessions: Gathering, Opening Worship, Conversation, and Conclusion.

OPENING WORSHIP

Prayer (unison)
O God, you love more than we can ever know. May your love be real to us, no matter where we have been or what we have done. Amen.

Lectio Divina (reflective or prayerful reading)
Read Ephesians 5:1–2 aloud. Invite all to reflect for a few minutes in silence.

After reflection time, invite all to listen for a word or phrase as the passage is read again and to reflect on that word or phrase in silence.

Read the passage a third time, asking all to offer a silent prayer following the reading.

Invite volunteers to share the word or phrase that spoke most deeply to them.

Prayer
Loving God, hear our prayers today as we seek to follow you more faithfully:
(spoken prayers may be offered)
O God, you have given us a pattern to follow in our lives. Help us to follow and especially to show love. Hear us now as we pray together, saying, Our Father . . .

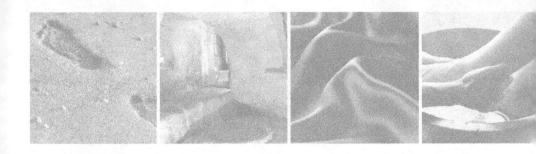

CONVERSATION

- Review the daily readings in "Loving" (pages 52–65). Share observations, reflections, and insights on the readings.
- Invite each member of the group briefly to reflect on ways their faith and love go together. Invite them to name ways their faith can be strengthened and ways they can live out love more fully. Then reflect on common themes or characteristics of their responses.
- Reflect on the following statement by Kendra Hotz: "The expansive scope of God's love in Jesus Christ means that all are invited, all are included." Ask: What are some of your reflections on that statement? What does it tell us about God? What are its implications for the church?
- Invite the group to name the human needs around them. Brainstorm some ways group members can try to meet these needs.

CONCLUSION

The Lord be with you.
   And also with you.
Sometimes it is hard to love others, O Christ. Make your love alive in us and help us love one another. Amen.

Hymn
"They'll Know We Are Christians by Our Love"

Thanking
(Fourth Week in Lent)

MAIN IDEA

Our Lenten journeys are steps of praise and thanks. We look always to the God who loves us in Jesus Christ. With Paul, we say, "Thanks be to God, who in Christ always leads us" (2 Corinthians 2:14).

PREPARING TO LEAD

- Read "Thanking (Fourth Week in Lent)" on pages 69–83.
- Read this study session and select questions and activities that you will use. What other questions, issues, or themes occur to you from your reflection?
- Each session includes a hymn. Provide copies of your congregation's hymnal. If you do not have a piano or keyboard and someone to play, consider asking someone to record the music to help the group sing the hymn.

GATHERING

- Provide name tags and pens as people arrive.
- Provide simple refreshments if other arrangements for refreshments have not been made; ask a volunteer to bring refreshments next week.
- Review the "ground rules" and logistics; e.g., time to begin and end the session; location for meetings; welcoming of all points

of view; confidentiality, etc. Encourage participants to bring their study books and Bibles.

- Review the format for these sessions: Gathering, Opening Worship, Conversation, and Conclusion.

OPENING WORSHIP

Prayer (unison)
We give thanks to you with our whole hearts, O Lord. We praise you! Amen.

Lectio Divina (reflective or prayerful reading)
Read Psalm 91 aloud. Invite all to reflect for a few minutes in silence.

After reflection time, invite all to listen for a word or phrase as the passage is read again and to reflect on that word or phrase in silence.

Read the passage a third time, asking all to offer a silent prayer following the reading.

Invite volunteers to share the word or phrase that spoke most deeply to them.

Prayer
Loving God, hear our prayers today as we seek to follow you more faithfully:
(spoken prayers may be offered)
We entrust ourselves to your care, O Jesus. Be with us, hold us, and keep us in your care. Hear us now as we pray together, saying, Our Father . . .

CONVERSATION

- Review the daily readings in "Thanking" (pages 70–83). Share observations, reflections, and insights on the readings.

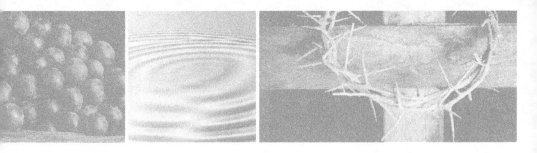

- Invite each member of the group briefly to name things for which he or she is grateful. Discuss the grace of God that provides the source of our gratitude. Then reflect on common themes or characteristics from these responses.
- Reflect on the following statement by Karl Barth: "Grace and gratitude belong together like heaven and earth. Grace evokes gratitude like the voice of an echo. Gratitude follows grace like thunder lightning. . . . The two belong together, so that only gratitude can correspond to grace, and this correspondence cannot fail." Ask: What are some of your reflections on the statement? What does it tell us about God?
- Invite the group to name ways in which their affections and actions are for the glory of God.

CONCLUSION

Prayer
The Lord be with you.
    And also with you.
May we live for your glory, O God, in all we think, say, and do.
Amen.

Hymn
"Now Thank We All Our God"

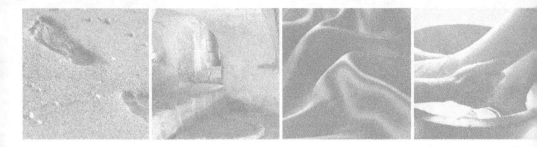

Enacting
(Fifth Week in Lent)

MAIN IDEA

Faith expresses itself in works. Our acting is inherent in our discipleship. Jesus led his early disciples into preaching, teaching, healing, and serving. He did not withdraw with his band of followers into a permanent retreat. He led them into ministries that brought glory to God and help to those in need.

PREPARING TO LEAD

- Read "Enacting (Fifth Week in Lent)" on pages 87–101.
- Read this study session and select questions and activities that you will use. What other questions, issues, or themes occur to you from your reflection?
- Each session includes a hymn. Provide copies of your congregation's hymnal. If you do not have a piano or keyboard and someone to play, consider asking someone to record the music to help the group sing the hymn.

GATHERING

- Provide name tags and pens as people arrive.
- Provide simple refreshments if other arrangements for refreshments have not been made; ask a volunteer to bring refreshments next week for a celebration of the group's time together.

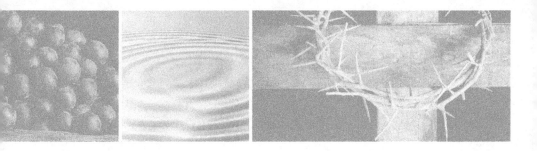

- Review the "ground rules" and logistics; e.g., time to begin and end the session; location for meetings; welcoming of all points of view; confidentiality, etc. Encourage participants to bring their study books and Bibles.
- Review the format for these sessions: Gathering, Opening Worship, Conversation, and Conclusion.

OPENING WORSHIP

Prayer (unison)
Stir us by your Spirit, O Christ, to love and serve you, now. Amen.

Lectio Divina (reflective or prayerful reading)
Read Mark 12:28–34 aloud. Invite all to reflect for a few minutes in silence.

After reflection time, invite all to listen for a word or phrase as the passage is read again and to reflect on that word or phrase in silence.

Read the passage a third time, asking all to offer a silent prayer following the reading.

Invite volunteers to share the word or phrase that spoke most deeply to them.

Prayer
Loving God, hear our prayers today as we seek to follow you more faithfully:
(spoken prayers may be offered)
We say we love you, O God. Help us to express our love for you by loving our neighbors—no matter who they are. Hear us now as we pray together, saying, Our Father . . .

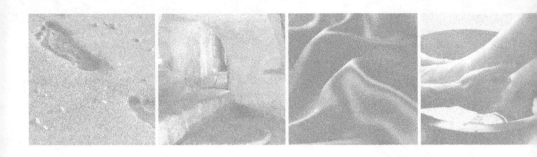

CONVERSATION

- Review the daily readings in "Enacting" (pages 88–101). Share observations, reflections, and insights on the readings.
- Invite members of the group to name things they do for Christ and the church. Ask: What motivates your actions? Then reflect on common themes or characteristics of their responses.
- Reflect on the following statement by Martin Luther: "We do not become righteous by doing righteous deeds but, having been made righteous, we do righteous deeds." Ask: What are some of your thoughts on the statement? What does it tell us about God?
- Invite the group to think of your church's activities in mission and ministry. Invite volunteers to name them and to describe how they help reconciliation take place.

CONCLUSION

Prayer

The Lord be with you.
    And also with you.
O God, you have reconciled us in Jesus Christ. Reenergize us as a community of reconciliation in a world where needs are great. Amen.

Hymn
"Called as Partners in Christ's Service"

Gathering at the Cross (Holy Week)

MAIN IDEA

As we contemplate dimensions of the cross, we find the wondrous drama of God's grace and love. The cross where the Son of God died for us brings us to the heart of our faith, for here the heart of God is given to us and for us. Here we see how much God loved the world and how much God loves us.

PREPARING TO LEAD

- Read "Gathering at the Cross (Holy Week)" on pages 105–119.
- Read this study session and select questions and activities that you will use. What other questions, issues, or themes occur to you from your reflection?
- Each session includes a hymn. Provide copies of your congregation's hymnal. If you do not have a piano or keyboard and someone to play, consider asking someone to record the music to help the group sing the hymn.
- This is the final group study session. Consider way to celebrate the completion of your shared Lenten discipline.

GATHERING

- Provide name tags and pens as people arrive.
- Review the "ground rules" and logistics; e.g., time to begin and

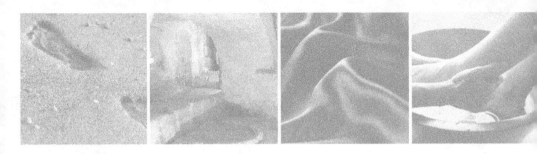

end the session; welcoming of all points of view; confidentiality, etc.

- Review the format for the session: Gathering, Opening Worship, Conversation, and Conclusion.

OPENING WORSHIP

Prayer (unison)
Lord Jesus Christ, thank you for giving your life for the world.
Thank you for giving your life for me. Amen.

Lectio Divina (reflective or prayerful reading)
Read Luke 23:32–38 aloud. Invite all to reflect for a few minutes in silence.

After reflection time, invite all to listen for a word or phrase as the passage is read again and to reflect on that word or phrase in silence.

Read the passage a third time, asking all to offer a silent prayer following the reading.

Invite volunteers to share the word or phrase that spoke most deeply to them.

Prayer
Loving God, hear our prayers today as we seek to follow you more faithfully:
(spoken prayers may be offered)
Bring us together in your love, O Christ. May hurts be healed and wholeness be found. Hear us now as we pray together, saying, Our Father . . .

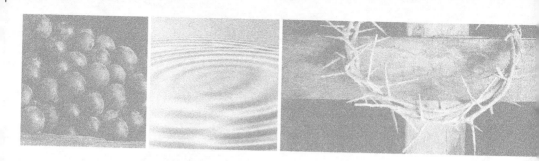

CONVERSATION

- Review the daily readings in "Gathering at the Cross" (pages 106–119). Share observations, reflections, and insights on the readings.
- Invite each member of the group briefly to discuss the forgiveness they have received through the death of Christ on the cross. Name ways to forgive others and to ask for forgiveness from others. Then reflect on common themes or characteristics of the responses.
- Reflect on the following statement by George Stroup: "All sound Christian theology begins and ends at the foot of the cross. It is the single event in the Gospels that unveils the full depth and horror of human sin and the radical nature of God's grace and love." Ask: What are some of your reflections on the statement? What does it tell us about God?
- Ask the group members how their participation in this study has strengthened their faith. Ask: What will you resolve to do based on your Lenten discipline?

CONCLUSION

Prayer
The Lord be with you.
    And also with you.
Thank you, Lord Jesus, for taking my judgment upon yourself and for giving me grace that overflows throughout my life. Amen.

Hymn
"O Sacred Head, Now Wounded"

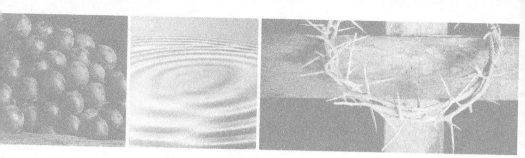

Notes on Quotes

1. **Jonathan Edwards (1703–1758)** was an important American theologian who was a pastor and, briefly, president of Princeton College.
2. **T. W. Manson (1893–1958)** was a British New Testament scholar who taught at the University of Manchester and was ordained in the Presbyterian Church of England.
3. **Hans Küng** is a contemporary theologian in the Roman Catholic tradition who has taught at the University of Tübingen and written a number of significant theological books.
4. **Dietrich Bonhoeffer (1906–1945)** was a German Lutheran pastor and theologian who was executed by the Nazis and was the author of important theological works.
5. **Gustavo Guttiérrez** is a Peruvian theologian and Dominican priest who is a leading, founding figure in liberation theology.
6. **John Calvin (1509–1564)** was a leading Protestant reformer who served in Geneva and is foundational for what became the Reformed theological tradition.
7. **William Ames (1576–1633)** was an English theologian who taught in the Netherlands and whose Reformed theological works were important for English and American Puritans.
8. **Frederick Buechner** is a contemporary novelist and theologian who explores the presence of God in everyday life.
9. **Wendy Farley** teaches in the Religion Department of Emory University and is the author of a number of stimulating theological books.
10. **John Calvin (1509–1564)** was a leading Protestant reformer who served in Geneva and is foundational for what became the Reformed theological tradition.

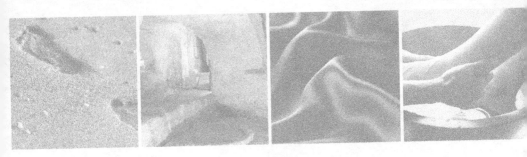

11. **A Brief Statement of Faith (1983)** is part of the *Book of Confessions* of the Presbyterian Church (U.S.A.).

12. **Donald G. Bloesch (1928–2010)** was a leading evangelical theologian whose many theological books drew widely from the historic Christian tradition.

13. **P. T. Forsyth (1848–1921)** was born in Scotland and was a Congregationalist theologian known for his many keen theological writings.

14. **Jürgen Moltmann** is a German theologian in the Reformed tradition whose many books have made him one of the world's leading theologians.

15. **Daniel L. Migliore** is an American Presbyterian theologian who taught for many years at Princeton Theological Seminary.

16. **Martha L. Moore-Keish** teaches theology at Columbia Theological Seminary in Decatur, Georgia.

17. **John Chrysostom (c. 347–407)** was archbishop of Constantinople and a leading preacher and theologian in the early church.

18. **Luise Schottroff** is a German theologian associated with the development of feminist theology.

19. **Augustine (354–430)** was bishop of Hippo Regius (now part of Algeria) and one of the most significant theologians of the early church period.

20. **Grace Ji-Sun Kim** teaches theology at the Moravian Theological Seminary in Bethlehem, Pennsylvania

21. **Kendra G. Hotz** teaches religious studies at Rhodes College in Memphis, Tennessee.

22. **William Perkins (1558–1602)** was an English Puritan theologian who wrote a number of important theological works.

23. **Augustine (354–430)** was bishop of Hippo Regius (now part of Algeria) and one of the most significant theologians of the early church period.

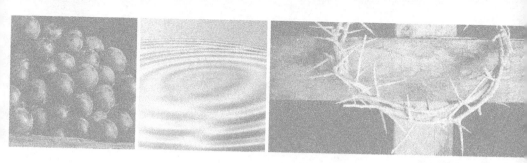

24. **Emilie M. Townes** teaches African American religion and theology at Yale Divinity School.

25. **Martin Luther (1483–1546)** was a German professor and theologian who helped initiate the Protestant Reformation and whose followers became known as Lutherans.

26. **Dietrich Bonhoeffer (1906–1945)** was a German Lutheran pastor and theologian who was executed by the Nazis and was the author of important theological works.

27. **Lisa Maugans Driver** teaches in the Department of Theology at Valparaiso University in Valparaiso, Indiana.

28. **Amy Plantinga Pauw** teaches theology at Louisville Presbyterian Theological Seminary in Louisville, Kentucky.

29. **Alan P. F. Sell** is a British theologian and professor who is the author of numerous important theological works.

30. **Karl Barth (1886–1968)** was one of the twentieth century's leading theologians whose vast writings continue to be significant today.

31. **Barbara Brown Taylor** is a well-known preacher and theologian who teaches religious studies at Piedmont College in Demorest, Georgia.

32. **John Downame (1571–1652)** was a British theologian whose theological works were well-regarded in his day.

33. **Gail R. O'Day** is dean and teaches New Testament and preaching at Wake Forest Divinity School in Winston-Salem, North Carolina.

34. **Martin Luther (1483–1546)** was a German professor and theologian who helped initiate the Protestant Reformation and whose followers became known as Lutherans.

35. **John Calvin (1509–1564)** was a leading Protestant reformer who served in Geneva and is foundational for what became the Reformed theological tradition.

36. **Henry G. Brinton** is pastor of Fairfax Presbyterian Church in Fairfax, Virginia.

37. **Jerome (c. 347–420)** is recognized as a Doctor of the Church in the Roman Catholic tradition and was translator of the Latin Vulgate as well as a theological writer.
38. **Karl Barth (1886–1968)** was one of the twentieth century's leading theologians whose vast writings continue to be significant today.
39. **The Confession of 1967** is part of the *Book of Confessions* of the Presbyterian Church (U.S.A.).
40. **Sally A. Brown** teaches preaching and worship at Princeton Theological Seminary in Princeton, New Jersey.
41. **Catherine Gunsalus González** taught church history at Columbia Theological Seminary in Decatur, Georgia, for a number of years.
42. **Donald M. Baillie (1887–1954)** was a Scots theologian in the Reformed tradition who taught at St. Mary's College of the University of St. Andrews in St. Andrews, Scotland.
43. **Andrew Sung Park** teaches theology and ethics at United Theological Seminary in Dayton, Ohio.
44. **William Sloane Coffin (1924–2006)** was a prominent preacher and social activist who was chaplain at Yale University and minister of the Riverside Church in New York City.
45. **Patricia Wilson-Kastner (1944–1998)** was an American pastor and theologian who taught preaching at several theological seminaries.
46. **George W. Stroup** teaches theology at Columbia Theological Seminary in Decatur, Georgia.

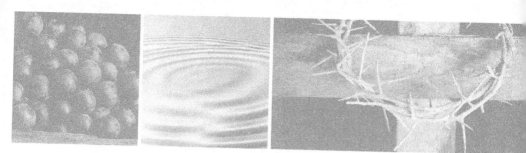

Endnotes

1. Jonathan Edwards, *The "Miscellanies,"* ed. Ava Chamberlain, *The Works of Jonathan Edwards* (New Haven: Yale University Press, 2000), 18:54–55.
2. T. W. Manson, *Ethics and the Gospel* (London: SCM Press, 1960), p. 68.
3. Hans Küng, *On Being a Christian*, trans. Edward Quinn (Garden City, N.Y.: Doubleday & Co., 1976), p. 281.
4. Dietrich Bonhoeffer, *The Cost of Discipleship*, trans. R. H. Fuller (New York: Macmillan, 1966), p. 41.
5. Gustavo Gutiérrez, *A Theology of Liberation*, trans. and ed. Sister Caridad Inda and John Eagleson (Maryknoll, N.Y.: Orbis Books, 1973), p. 154.
6. John Calvin, "The Catechism of the Church of Geneva" (1541) in *The School of Faith*, ed. and trans. Thomas F. Torrance (New York: Harper & Brothers Publishers, 1959), p. 5.
7. William Ames, *The Marrow of Theology*, trans. John Dykstra Eusden (Boston: Pilgrim Press, 1968), p. 80. The Mark Twain quote is from Mark Twain, *Following the Equator*, part 2: chap. 12, "Pudd'nhead Wilson's New Calendar" (1897).
8. Frederick Buechner, *Wishful Thinking* (New York: Harper & Row, 1973), p. 40.
9. Wendy Farley, *The Wounding and Healing of Desire* (Louisville, Ky.: Westminster John Knox Press, 2005), p. 72.
10. John Calvin, *The Second Epistle of Paul to the Corinthians, and the Epistles to Timothy, Titus and Philemon*, trans. T. A. Smail, *Calvin's New Testament Commentaries*, ed. David W. Torrance and Thomas F. Torrance, rpt. (Grand Rapids: Eerdmans, 1974), 10:77, *Commentary on 2 Corinthians 5:18*.
11. *A Brief Statement of Faith*, *Book of Confessions: Study Edition* (Louisville, Ky.: Geneva Press, 1996), 10.1.
12. Donald G. Bloesch, *Theological Notebook: Volume III: 1969–1983*, The Spiritual Journals of Donald G. Bloesch, rpt. (Eugene, Ore.: Wipf & Stock, 2005), p. 235.
13. P. T. Forsyth, *The Soul of Prayer* (Vancouver, British Columbia: Regent College Publishing, 2002), p. 74.
14. Jürgen Moltmann, "Praying with Open Eyes" in Jürgen Moltmann and Elisabeth Moltmann-Wendel, *Passion for God: Theology in Two Voices* (Louisville, Ky.: Westminster John Knox Press, 2003), p. 57.
15. Daniel L. Migliore, *The Power of God and the gods of Power* (Louisville, Ky.: Westminster John Knox Press, 2008), p. 110.
16. Martha L. Moore-Keish, *Christian Prayer for Today* (Louisville, Ky.: Westminster John Knox Press, 2009), p. 65.
17. John Chrysostom, *Homilies on 1 Timothy* in Nicene and Post-Nicene Fathers, ed. Philip Schaff (New York: Charles Scribner's Sons, 1905), homily 6 on 1 Timothy 2:1–4, 13:426.
18. Luise Schottroff, *Lydia's Impatient Sisters: A Feminist Social History of Early Christianity* (Louisville, Ky.: Westminster John Knox Press, 1995), p. 102.

19. Augustine, *Augustine: Confessions and Enchiridion*, ed. and trans. Albert C. Outler, The Library of Christian Classics, ed. John Baillie, John T. McNeill, and Henry P. Van Dusen (Philadelphia: Westminster Press, 1955), 7:47.
20. Grace Ji-Sun Kim, "1 John 3:1–3," *Feasting on the Word*, year A, vol. 4, ed. David L. Bartlett and Barbara Brown Taylor (Louisville, Ky.: Westminster John Knox Press, 2011), p. 232.
21. Kendra G. Hotz, "Isaiah 60:1–6," *Feasting on the Word*, year C, vol. 1, ed. David L. Bartlett and Barbara Brown Taylor (Louisville, Ky.: Westminster John Knox Press, 2009), p. 198.
22. William Perkins, "A Commentary on the 11th Chapter of the Hebrews," *The Workes of William Perkins*, 3 vols. (Cambridge: John Legatte, 1616–1618), 3:59.
23. Augustine, *Homilies on the Gospel of John*, Nicene and Post-Nicene Fathers (New York: Christian Literature Co., 1892), tractate 65, 2 (on John 13:34–35), 1:318.
24. Emilie M. Townes, "Mark 12:38–44," *Feasting on the Word*, year B, vol. 4, ed. David L. Bartlett and Barbara Brown Taylor (Louisville, Ky.: Westminster John Knox Press, 2011), p. 288.
25. Martin Luther, "Preface" to "Ordinance of a Common Chest" (1523), *The Christian in Society*, vol. 2, ed. Walther I. Brandt, Luther's Works (Philadelphia: Fortress Press, 1962), 45:172.
26. Dietrich Bonhoeffer, "Better Than Life Itself," *No Rusty Swords: Letters, Lectures and Notes 1928–1936 from the Collected Works*, vol.1, ed. Edwin H. Robertson, trans. John Bowden in conjunction with Pastor Bethge, rpt. (London: Collins, 1970), p. 125.
27. Lisa D. Maugans Driver, "Psalm 146," *Feasting on the Word*, year B, vol. 4, ed. David L. Bartlett and Barbara Brown Taylor (Louisville, Ky.: Westminster John Knox Press, 2011), p. 248.
28. Amy Plantinga Pauw, "Romans 8:6–11," *Feasting on the Word*, year A, vol. 2, ed. David L. Bartlett and Barbara Brown Taylor (Louisville, Ky.: Westminster John Knox Press, 2011), p. 138.
29. Alan P. F. Sell, *Christ Our Savior: Doctrine and Devotion* (Shippensburg, Pa.: Ragged Edge Press, 2000), p. 108.
30. Karl Barth, *Church Dogmatics*, trans. G. W. Bromiley, ed. G. W. Bromiley and T. F. Torrance, 13 vols. (New York: Charles Scribner's Sons, 1956), IV/1, 41.
31. Barbara Brown Taylor, *Leaving Church* (San Francisco: HarperSanFrancisco, 2007), p. 218.
32. John Downame, *A Guide to Godlinesse* (London, 1622), p. 13.
33. Gail R. O'Day, "John," *Women's Bible Commentary: Expanded Edition*, ed. Carol A. Newsom and Sharon H. Ringe (Louisville, Ky.: Westminster John Knox Press, 1998), p. 388.
34. Martin Luther, "Disputation Against Scholastic Theology," *The Career of the Reformer*, vol. 1, ed. Harold J. Grimm and Helmut T. Lehmann, Luther's Works (Philadelphia: Fortress Press, 1957), 31:10, no. 40.

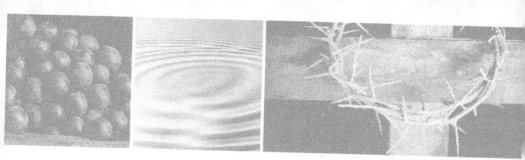

35. John Calvin, *Institutes of the Christian Religion,* trans. Ford Lewis Battles, ed. John T. McNeill, Library of Christian Classics (Philadelphia: Westminster Press, 1960), 3.3.20.

36. Henry G. Brinton, *Stewardship of Creation,* part of *Being Reformed: Faith Seeking Understanding* curriculum (Louisville, Ky.: Congregational Ministries Publishing, Presbyterian Church (U.S.A.), 2010), p. 8.

37. Jerome, "Homily 55 on Psalm 145 (146)" in *The Homilies of Saint Jerome,* vol. 1, trans. Marie Liguori Ewald, Fathers of the Church (Washington, D.C.: Catholic University of America Press, 1964), p. 393.

38. Karl Barth, *Church Dogmatics,* trans. G. W. Bromiley, ed. G. W. Bromiley and T. F. Torrance, rpt. (Edinburgh: T&T Clark, 1967), IV/2:810.

39. The Confession of 1967, *Book of Confessions: Study Edition* (Louisville, Ky.: Geneva Press, 1996), 9.31 (Inclusive Language Text).

40. Sally A. Brown, *Cross Talk: Preaching Redemption Here and Now* (Louisville, Ky.: Westminster John Knox Press, 2008), p. 118.

41. Catherine Gunsalus González, *1 & 2 Peter and Jude,* Belief: A Theological Commentary on the Bible (Louisville, Ky.: Westminster John Knox Press, 2010), p. 146.

42. Donald M. Baillie, *God Was in Christ: An Essay on Incarnation and Atonement,* rpt. (London: Faber and Faber, 1963), p. 189.

43. Andrew Sung Park, *Triune Atonement: Christ's Healing for Sinners, Victims, and the Whole Creation* (Louisville, Ky.: Westminster John Knox Press, 2009), p. 91.

44. William Sloane Coffin, *The Collected Sermons of William Sloane Coffin: The Riverside Years,* vol. 1 (Louisville, Ky.: Westminster John Knox Press, 2008), p. 26.

45. Patricia Wilson-Kastner, *Faith, Feminism, and the Christ* (Philadelphia: Fortress Press, 1983), p. 100.

46. George W. Stroup, *Why Jesus Matters* (Louisville, Ky.: Westminster John Knox Press, 2011), p. 68.

Endnotes